SPRAY & STITCH

The Chinese Vase with Anemones picture shows how effectively the techniques of spray painting and cross stitch embroidery can be combined. You will have to look hard to spot the sprayed flowers amongst the stitched ones! Full instructions for working this project can be found on page 89.

SPRAY & STITCH

OVER 30 PROJECTS COMBINING CROSS STITCH
WITH EASY SPRAY PAINT TECHNIQUES

SALLY HARMAN

David & Charles

DEDICATION

For R, whose love and friendship are
inspiration for everything I achieve

ACKNOWLEDGEMENTS

This book has required more development time than a conventional cross stitch book and I am therefore especially grateful to those who have supported it through to publication, in particular my former agent, Doreen Montgomery. Cheryl Brown at David & Charles has given generously the fullest support possible any author could wish for. Brenda Morrison, Linda Clements and Kit Johnson have all greatly assisted with the process of squeezing the book's contents into the space available. The yarns and fabric were generously supplied by DMC Creative World and Cara Ackerman and Susan Shanks of DMC have both provided excellent assistance of different kinds. My thanks also go to Jane, Adam and Phil at DMC. The Clock, Trays and other finished items were all supplied by Framecraft Miniatures and special thanks go to Sarah Gray at Framecraft.

Hands-on help has been provided by Sue, Margarethe and Jean. Other practical assistance and support has been provided by Rebecca, Tess and David. John Jay and his staff, especially Dominic, have helped with specialised copying requirements. Finally, I would like to thank Lyn Le Grice for providing wonderful workshops which ensured I acquired the stencil-making skills essential to the foundation of this book.

A DAVID & CHARLES BOOK

First published in the UK in 1997

Copyright © Sally Harman 1997
Photography by David Johnson

Sally Harman has asserted her right to be identified as author of this work in accordance with the Copyright, Designs and Patents Act, 1988.

A catalogue record for this book is available from the British Library.

ISBN 0 7153 0460 7

Photographs by David Johnson
Styling by Kit Johnson
Book design by Kit Johnson
Illustrations by Sally Harman
Printed in the USA

for David & Charles
Brunel House   Newton Abbot   Devon

CONTENTS

INTRODUCTION

There is no shortage of books on cross stitch and they usually have either a specific design theme or a common end-use purpose. This book is different in that it covers a wide range of projects and also introduces a much-needed new dimension to working in cross stitch. The principle is simple in that it combines the easiest of stencil making approaches with the quickest of painting techniques and uses them as a foundation for cross stitch. Furthermore, this book has been created for all stitchers, whatever their skills or abilities. No drawing skills are required as all the outlines for the stencils are provided – you simply photocopy them onto card, cut them out and then spray and stitch.

The spray paints are easy to use, quick (they dry instantly), and impressive results are obtainable by the least artistic individual. Many people are put off by the whole idea of stencilling either because it is too fiddly or messy, too time consuming or they had unsuccessful results in the past. By using aerosol paints all these difficulties are avoided. The techniques of spray painting are clearly explained and illustrated in step-by-step instructions. The only problem is that you may want to use aerosol paints on everything from plant pots to walls!

This exciting new dimension to cross stitch has many advantages. Apart from the obvious aesthetic benefits, it allows large pieces of work to be created in a similar time to smaller conventional pieces. The Kitty Bag on page 106 takes very little time to complete because most of the design area is covered by the kitten stencil. As well as saving time, this combination technique allows no chance of boredom creeping into the work as large areas of colour are sprayed rather than stitched.

Another advantage of combining spray paint with needlework is the added visual depth, subtlety and texture which results. The Pond Picture on page 116 and the Leafy Tray on page 110 are good examples of how the combination achieves effects only possible by adding subtle colour to needlework. Also, a more painterly feel is created by the added perspective and by the curves and sloping lines which, if stitched, would be stepped or stilted.

Circles and curved shapes have always presented a problem for cross-stitch designers for unless you are working on the finest of fabrics it is impossible to achieve a perfect circle. The curved lines of the Sun Cushion on page 94 and the Sculpture Garden Tray on page 68 are more naturalistic for being produced by paint rather than stitching.

As well as introducing this new dimension to working in cross stitch, this book also presents different approaches to finishing needlework items. This includes covering mounts and frames with decorative paper and spray painting trays, frames and clocks. There is no reason why spray paint cannot be used to decorate a frame or other item to complement the stitched piece. In this way, you can achieve a more creative and individual piece of work and gain great satisfaction in the process.

Information about the basic materials and equipment you will need follows. After this is the exciting bit – a clear and highly illustrated description of how to achieve the various spray painting and stencilling effects. Beginners, in particular, will want to read the stitching section which covers the method of stitching and the stitches used. At the end of the project work, on page 126, there is a short section on framing your embroidery. You will then be more than ready to spray and stitch!

MATERIALS AND EQUIPMENT

FABRICS

It is possible to work cross stitch on a wide variety of fabrics as well as paper, netting and plastic. Most of the projects in the book use Aida, an evenweave fabric, but a quarter of the designs are worked on linen. Linen is easy to use but if you wish you can substitute 14 count Aida for 28 count linen.

Whatever fabric you use it is important to purchase the best quality available. If you are going to spend time and effort on a piece of work it seems appropriate to use good quality materials. Not only will the finished piece look better, it will also wash and wear better.

Aida and Aida Plus

Aida is the easiest fabric to use as it has clearly defined stitch holes. This makes it not only easy for stitching but also for counting stitches or spaces. In addition, the firm structure of the fabric ensures your stitching will retain a regular appearance.

Aida is available in a variety of 'count' sizes. A 'count' number of 14 means that the fabric has 14 stitches per inch (2.5cm) if each stitch is worked across the space between one hole and the next. Similarly, 18 count means there are 18 holes per inch (2.5cm) and thereby 18 stitches per inch (2.5cm). It follows that the higher the count number, the smaller the stitch and the finer the work; thus, 11 count is a larger stitch and useful for bigger pieces.

Aida Plus is a relatively new concept and has been used for the Striped Picture Frame and the Kitty Bag. It is a non-fraying Aida fabric sold in single sheet packs measuring 9 x 12in (23 x 30cm). If you are unable to obtain this you can create a similar fabric yourself by backing Aida with iron-on lining fabric prior to spraying.

Linen

Linen is an openweave fabric and the width of the threads can vary so a frame must be used to ensure even stitching. The count size of linen refers to the number of threads per inch (2.5cm), therefore 28 count means 28 threads per inch (2.5cm), measured horizontally or vertically. It is possible to produce extremely fine work by taking one thread per stitch but usually two threads per stitch are used, creating 14 stitches per inch (2.5cm). In this book, where 28 count linen is used, readers can substitute 14 count Aida for some, but not all, of the designs. However, different types of linen come in different thread counts so it is important to ensure you have purchased the right count fabric.

Evenweave

This is an all-cotton fabric with the same structure as linen. It is evenly woven and, unlike linen, each thread is of equal thickness, giving a stable fabric. Evenweave is only used for the Arabian Camels Picture.

THREADS

In the same way that a variety of materials can be used for cross stitch, a wide range of threads can also be used, including silk, raffia or ribbon. The threads used in this book are those readily available from good needlework shops.

DMC Stranded Embroidery Cotton (Floss)

This is the most widely available and versatile thread. It is loosely-twisted with six strands and a high-lustre finish. It is best used in short lengths and for the designs in this book it is divided and used as either one, two or three strands.

DMC Medicis Crewel Embroidery Wool

This is a beautiful soft yarn and is suitable for pieces where a different texture is required, such as the Edward Bear Pen-Case or where a piece is likely to be handled frequently.

DMC Flower Thread

This is a non-mercerised cotton with a matt finish and as such is very suitable for the bark of the Flowering Bonsai Pictures. One strand of Flower thread is roughly equivalent to two strands of embroidery cotton (floss).

DMC Metallic Thread

This is usually sold on a reel and is a triple-strand thread. It can easily be untwisted and separated so that the individual strands can be used on their own or in pairs. However, in this book it is used straight from the reel and a length is folded double for stitching.

NEEDLES

In order to work cross stitch on the fabrics used in this book it is important to use tapestry needles rather than embroidery needles. A tapestry needle has a blunt end so that it can pass between fabric threads without catching or splitting any of the fabric's fibres and entangling the yarn threads. It also ensures that the embroidery thread is not split when a needle is brought from the reverse side of the fabric to the front alongside an existing stitch.

The most commonly used needles are sizes 20 and 22. It is important to make sure your needle does not distort the size of the stitching holes of the fabric, so choose a smaller size needle if in doubt. It is useful to have several needles so that if you do not use all of a length of thread in one area of stitching, that needle can be put to one side awaiting the need for that colour again. This avoids unthreading and re-threading yarn, both saving time and reducing the chance of the thread losing its lustre.

HOOPS AND FRAMES

Embroidery Hoops

Most of the designs in this book are larger than average so a tapestry frame is more useful than an embroidery hoop. However, if you do use a hoop, make sure it is large enough to avoid any spray-painted areas being in contact with it. There are two reasons for this: it is difficult to remove creases from spray-painted areas and crushing the sprayed fabric between the two parts of the hoop will loosen the fine droplets of paint, making the fabric appear faded.

Rotating Frames

These are more useful as they are adjustable and can accommodate larger pieces of work. Available in different widths, they allow the excess fabric to be rolled up on the rotating sides of the frame, leaving the area to be worked flat and quite taut. Choose a frame which will accommodate your fabric but is not overwide as it could be cumbersome. For some pieces a quilting frame would be a suitable alternative. If you wish to stitch several projects it is worth trying to purchase a table-mounted frame. A free-standing (floor) frame is not recommended but if you are used to working on one and do not suffer any spinal discomfort then continue to use it.

SCISSORS

It is important to use sharp, small-bladed scissors for cutting out the stencils but you will also find it helpful to have a good pair of embroidery scissors for cutting thread.

AIR-SOLUBLE PEN

This pen usually produces a purple line which fades after a short time. It is most important not to confuse it with embroidery marker pens (which often also produce a purple line but are permanent or semi-permanent).

SPRAY PAINTING AND STENCILLING

Some readers may have attempted stencil-making and stencilling before, with varying degrees of success: others will perhaps have been put off the idea of stencilling because they have felt it to be either time-consuming or intimidating. This book will introduce you to a very quick method of stencilling (using spray paints), and the stencil-making (using the outlines given, photocopied onto card) could not be simpler. Most of the designs use stencils which can, with the exception of the Celtic Circle, be cut out with sharp scissors. (The Celtic Circle can be cut out with scissors but it is more easily prepared using a craft knife.)

Various other materials are used to create stencil effects or to mask off areas of fabric. These include masking tape, double-sided adhesive tape and string. For example, the Delft Tile Wall Hanging uses double-sided adhesive tape and a light covering of Royal Blue paint is sprayed either side of the lines of tape. When the tape is removed it reveals the white areas to give the impression of grouting. Larger areas can be blocked, for example as in the Rose Trellis Cushion. Clear plastic is used but the masking is illustrated with green adhesive-backed felt so that the masking can easily be seen. In the Striped Picture Frame, string is used for the masking.

MAKING THE CARD STENCILS

The majority of the outlines provided will fit onto a single piece of A4 or A3 card. Your photocopy shop will know the thickness of card their machine will take but, if you are buying the card separately, make sure it is at least 160g and not more than 230g. Check the photo-

copier you use can cope with at least 160g.

In a few cases the image required will be larger than A3 so it is photocopied onto two A3 sheets, with sufficient overlap where the pieces of card are to be joined. To join, place the centre edge of one card on top of the centre edge of the other, fitting the pieces side by side. Place two small pieces of masking tape on the front of the card to secure the position, then flip the cards over and stick masking tape along the length of the join. Turn the card over and remove the tape used to hold the cards in position. You can then cut out the stencil.

CUTTING THE STENCILS

The card used at photocopying shops is sufficiently thick for a stencil that can be used five or six times yet is thin enough to be cut

To cut out a stencil, pierce a hole in the centre of the card with a sharp scissor point and cut towards the edge of the design.

easily with sharp scissors. Avoid cutting with blunt scissors as the fibres of the card will not have neat edges and a blurred stencil outline will result. The best way to cut out a piece of the stencil is to carefully make a small hole with the scissor point, and cut towards the edge of a piece of design. Then cut all around the edge of the printed design. If you accidentally cut the card in the wrong place, simply stick masking tape on the reverse side of the card to repair it.

APPLYING THE STENCILS

It is important for the finished effect to position the stencil correctly on the fabric and the instructions for each project will tell you how to do this. For most of the projects, it is also essential to have good contact with the fabric you are spraying, otherwise the edges of the sprayed areas will be blurred and distorted. This effect can be used deliberately for a design where this is suitable but most rely on a crisp, clean line of spraying and using Spray Mount adhesive is the easiest method of achieving this.

Spray Mount Adhesive
This is a temporary glue which allows for repositioning and gives good contact with fabric. It is not used on all the designs in this book but is essential for most. Read the manufacturer's instructions before using the adhesive. A light spray on the reverse side of the stencil card is best. If you spray too heavily, the glue will remain over-tacky and difficulties will result if any adhesive sits on the surface of the fabric to be stitched.

Masking Tape
This is extremely useful for mending card and attaching scrap card to the outer edges of a stencil to protect fabric which is to be kept free from paint. It is better than ordinary adhesive tape as it allows the card to be re-used without renewing the tape.

To ensure good contact, lightly spray the reverse of the stencil with Spray Mount before positioning onto the fabric. Then tape scrap card to the outer edges of the stencil to protect the rest of the fabric before spraying.

In some designs masking tape is used as a stencil itself, for example, in the Delft Tile Wall Hanging, where masking tape or a stronger, double-sided adhesive tape is used for the stencilled lines to imitate grouting.

PAINTS

Types of Paint Used
All the paints used in this book are ozone friendly (CFC-free) aerosol spray paints, readily available from various stores. Two types of paint are used; fast-drying spray enamel paints (available in small cans) and professional car touch-up paints (available in 300ml cans). For suppliers information see page 127.

The various enamel colours used are as follows: Teal, Peach, Turquoise, Lavender, Sunshine Yellow, Sky Blue, Rose, Parrot Green and Gold Leaf. The car touch-up paints used (abbreviated to their colour name only in the materials list of each project) were Rover Solar Yellow, Vauxhall Leaf Green, Peugeot Black, Peugeot Royal Blue, Ford Jasmine

Yellow, Ford Highland Green, Ford Sunburst Red, Ford Dove Grey, Ford Ceramic Blue and Ford Tuscan Beige.

LONG-TERM CARE OF SPRAYED PROJECTS

Although some of the projects in this book are framed pictures or trays and will therfore not require regular cleaning, many designs are likely to be handled and become soiled. Follow the three steps below and your finished piece will keep its fresh appearance.

1 Always wash an item when it is lightly soiled – it is better to wash gently on a regular basis than to wait until a piece is heavily soiled.

2 Use a washing liquid specially formulated for embroidery (sachets of this are available from all good needlework shops) and follow the manufacturer's instructions. Dry the laundered piece flat. Iron while it is still damp.

3 Place a sheet of clean paper over the reverse side of the stitching and a damp cloth on top of that. Iron on a medium hot setting. If you are ironing calico or linen you may need to re-dampen the fabric in order to remove all the creases.

PREPARATION FOR SPRAYING

In addition to the manufacturer's health and safety information and to the advice outlined in the Using Your Paints Safely box below, it is important to prepare for spraying and to carry out test spraying on scrap paper before you begin any of the projects in this book. The fine mist spray of these paints can cover an area much larger than you intend to spray. It is therefore vital to protect your work surface and surrounding vicinity by covering with an easily removable, disposable covering. I use clean, unused, newspaper-quality paper, available in A1 size. Used computer print-out paper and lining paper are good substitutes. When you are sure you have fully protected everything necessary, assemble the paint(s), scrap paper (for test spraying), Spray Mount adhesive, scrap card and masking tape (if being used for the project) and have the cut stencil to hand.

Health and Safety Information
It is **extremely important** to use and store the paints in accordance with the manufacturer's instructions.

USING YOUR SPRAY PAINTS SAFELY

- ◆ **Keep paints out of reach of children and animals.**

- ◆ **Keep paint away from any sources of ignition – no smoking.**

- ◆ **Shake the can well before use.**

- ◆ **Protect your face, in particular your air passages, with either a disposable mask or metal mask with replaceable gauze.**

- ◆ **Use only in well-ventilated areas.**

- ◆ **Store and dispose of used cans in accordance with the manufacturer's instructions.**

TEST SPRAYING

Most projects require a fine mist or a build-up of light sprayings and you will need to test spray each time you use a colour. This is best done on scrap paper prior to using the paint on fabric. For all spraying, except spotting (see page 16), the can needs to be shaken well to achieve a good mist of paint. Hold the can approximately 8in (20cm) away from the surface you are spraying and use a series of short bursts of spraying.

Test spraying not only provides spraying practice, it also increases your confidence in using the paints, and allows you to identify any problems with clogged nozzles. (The car spray paints usually have anti-clog nozzles but the nozzle of an enamel paint can may occasionally clog up.) To free a clogged nozzle, shake the can well, hold it upside down and spray against a piece of scrap card. If it remains clogged you can either remove a nozzle from another can and substitute it for the clogged one, or remove it and try to clean it with white spirit. To do this, remove the nozzle and immerse it in a small amount of white spirit. (Nail polish remover can be used as an alternative to white spirit.) The clogged paint should soften in the spirit and can be gently removed with either cotton wool or a soft brush. When you replace the nozzle a small amount of paint may spray out, so take care that the point of the nozzle is directed towards a piece of scrap paper.

When you are happy with the spraying quality, the next stage is to test your stencil on scrap paper. This allows you to correct any errors or omissions in cutting out the card and revealed after spraying. With a complicated stencil it is quite easy to overlook small areas which need cutting out. Do not apply Spray Mount adhesive for the test spraying. If you do need to cut out any part of the stencil it would be very difficult to do so if your card is tacky with adhesive. If after test spraying you find that you have removed too much card when

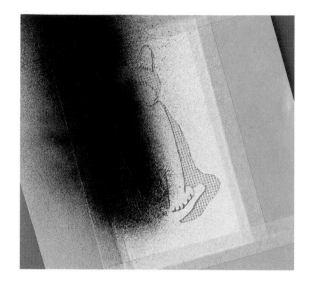

Once the stencil has been carefully positioned and the outer edges of the fabric masked with scrap card, you are ready to begin spray painting. Shake the can well and, holding it approximately 8in (20cm) away from the fabric, spray in short bursts.

cutting out the stencil, you can repair this by attaching a small piece of card with masking tape and correctly re-cutting the stencil.

PREPARATION FOR SPRAYING THE FABRIC

After successful test spraying, and making sure the paint on your stencil has dried, you can proceed to spray the fabric. This should be crease-free and placed on a flat surface. It is important that the fabric is crease-free prior to spraying as the sprayed areas cannot easily be ironed afterwards.

The next step is to position your stencil on the fabric. Stencils are normally placed in the centre of the fabric but there are exceptions so check the project instructions before spraying. Most, but not all, stencils require Spray Mount adhesive to be applied to the reverse side. For some projects you will be applying this prior to removing any fabric creases. This is to allow a short amount of time for the adhesive to lose more of its tackiness, reducing the level of

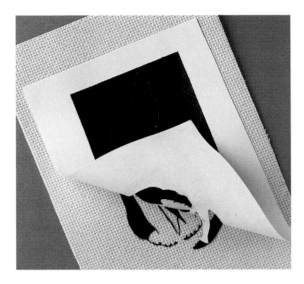

Once you have applied the spray paint evenly across the stencil, you can remove the scrap card and carefully

peel away the stencil (above left) to reveal the sprayed image (above right).

residue likely to be retained by the fabric, but still give good contact with the fabric. (Too much adhesive transferred onto the fabric will not only make stitching difficult but it could also damage the sewing thread or cause it to lose its sheen.)

DENSITY OF SPRAY AND COVERAGE

It is important to obtain the correct density of spraying and coverage. These are best achieved by a series of short bursts of spray. The instructions for individual projects will indicate whether light or more dense coverage is required. Irrespective of the kind of coverage, you will need to shake the paint can again just before spraying the fabric. (All the paints used in this book dry virtually instantaneously on the fabric so you do not have to wait for a light spraying to dry before applying another.)

Light Coverage
This is used for pieces like the Terrace Pots Bag which require a fine mist or hint of colour rather than a single solid block of a shade. It is always better to underspray rather than over-

spray a piece. You can easily add more paint but you cannot remove it from fabric without risking damaging the fabric's fibres. It is surprising just how little paint is required to achieve a light coverage and the test spraying of the stencil onto paper will help you get it right when spraying the fabric. If in doubt, always underspray.

Solid Coverage
This is used for projects like the Elephant Family Picture and the Arabian Camels Picture, which both require a solid expanse of colour. It is better to spray the area lightly and then gradually add further light sprays. This ensures that paint does not spread to areas where it is not desired. Also, openweave fabrics such as linen require less paint to give solid coverage than more closely woven fabric such as Aida.

If the area to be sprayed is small, as in Sample 1 (page 14), the length of each burst should be of

The spray painted samplers on the following pages show the different effects it is possible to achieve with spray painting. It is a good idea to test spray before beginning the projects in this book.

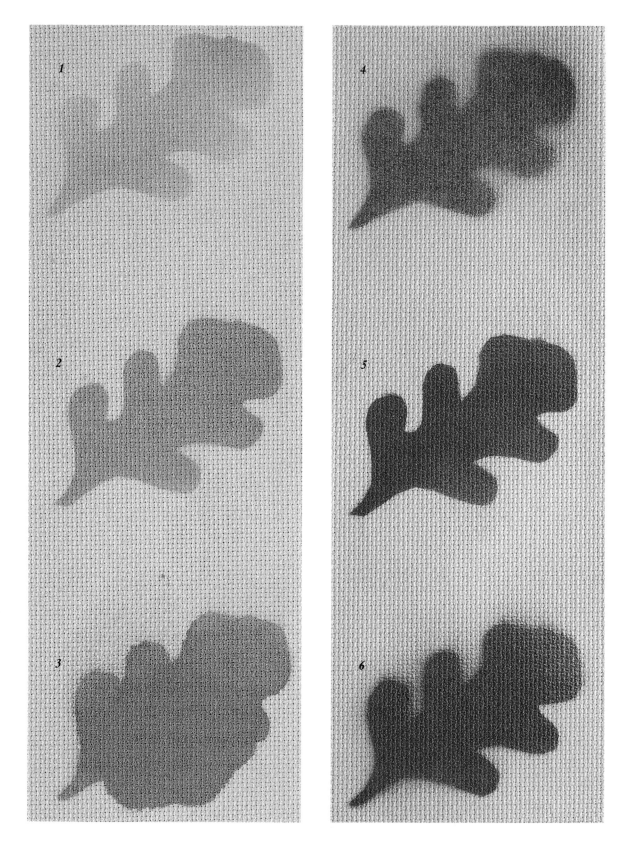

Samples 1–3 *Different spraying densities.*

Samples 4–6 *Achieving soft and crisp edges.*

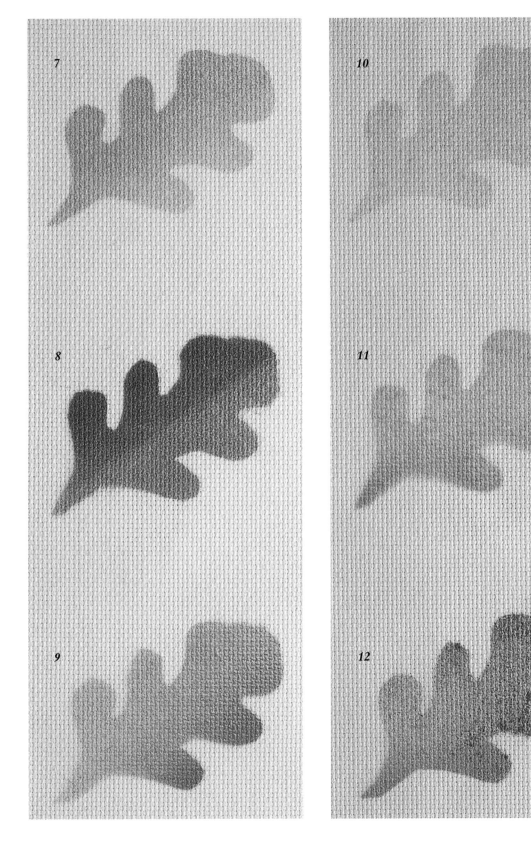

7

8

9

10

11

12

Samples 7–9 Creating shadow.

Samples 10–12 Creating texture.

a 1 second duration, with the nozzle fully depressed. Repeat this several times to achieve a solid coverage, as in sample 2. Sample 3 shows what will result if the paint is applied in a single, long burst of spraying. The fabric cannot absorb the paint and it does not have the chance to dry before more paint lands onto it so paint bleeds under the stencil.

Soft, Blurred Edges

Some subjects look better with a soft edge to their outline and this is achieved by placing a stencil onto fabric without first applying Spray Mount adhesive to its reverse side. The Pond Picture shows how soft edges give a more 'natural' look to a piece. To achieve this it is essential that the stencil card should be flat and not curled or bent in any way. This will ensure regular, even but 'loose' contact with the fabric and sample 4 illustrates this. When you spray the paint, try to ensure that the can's length is held parallel to the fabric to avoid paint drifting too much under the card.

Hard, Sharp Edges

For most designs it is essential to have a hard, sharp edge to the image. The Edwardian Silhouette Picture and the Iceland Poppies Clock are good examples of this type of edge. To achieve this, it is essential to ensure the edges of the stencil are cut with very sharp scissors. The other essential point is that the stencil should make good contact with the fabric at all points along the cut edges of the card. This is achieved by giving the cut edges of the stencil an even coat of Spray Mount adhesive and by working on a firm, flat surface, pressing the stencil gently onto the fabric. Use a finger to firm the edges of the stencil and apply steady pressure to achieve good contact, as shown in sample 5. Too much pressure could result in the stencil lifting elsewhere along the edges. Sample 6 shows the result when only partial contact is made.

SPRAY PAINT EFFECTS

Note: For all the spray paint effects that follow you will be using the equivalent of two or more colours. It is therefore important to bear in mind that unless you apply each colour with a light spray, and build up the spraying slowly, the combined volume of paint could saturate the fabric, resulting in overspraying and leakage.

Creating Shadow

Shadows can be created in two ways and have the benefit of adding depth and realism to a piece. You can either use a second, darker colour to create shadows in specific parts, as in the Terrace Pots Bag. Alternatively, you can use the same colour, as for the vase in the Chinese Vase with Anemones. In the vase, the shadow effect also adds definition to the shape of the vase and indicates the light source of the picture. For both methods, the first step is to spray the first colour very lightly, as in sample 7.

To create a shadow using a darker colour, the spray will need to be directed at specific parts of the coloured area. This can be done by aiming the second colour at the stencil card and then gradually moving your aim towards the required area, or by holding a piece of scrap card at an angle to the fabric to create a barrier and thus protect part of the area from the second colour (see sample 8).

For a more subtle form of shadow, a single colour is used and the shadow is created by allowing subsequent sprayings to drift across part of the fabric to produce the effect shown in sample 9. This is achieved by first aiming the nozzle at the stencil card adjacent to where the shadow is required and then gradually altering the direction of the spray so that it drifts across the relevant part of the design.

Creating Texture

Texture, such as that used in the Sculpture Garden Tray, can be created by using two or more colours and two different spraying techniques. To illustrate this two colours have been used in combination with a second technique (which uses a third colour). First, spray the first colour lightly, as in sample 10. The second colour is applied as in sample 11. (More colours can be added at this stage providing they remain distinct and subsequent colours do not obliterate earlier ones.) The final colour (or your second colour if using only two) is added using a spotting technique. Nozzles of spray cans vary slightly so it is important to experiment on scrap paper first to see which of the two techniques described below works best. Sample 12 shows the desired effect.

- ‘Spotting’ can be achieved by *not* shaking the can before use.
- ‘Spotting’ can be achieved by applying *uneven* pressure to the nozzle during spraying.

Free-Style Spraying

This approach can be used to create shadow and texture in the same piece, as well as producing a more individualistic and personal piece. The Leafy Tray and Pond Picture are examples of this but the Beach Sunset Picture shows the full potential of this type of spraying. It is also a useful technique for creating depth and perspective. It is explained more fully in the relevant project instructions.

STITCHING AND STITCHES

STARTING AND FINISHING

To start, cut a length of thread about 18in (45.5cm), thread the specified number of strands through your needle and tie a knot in one end. Insert the needle down into the front of the fabric 1in (2.5cm) away from your intended first stitch and in the direction you will be working. The knot should be on the front of your work. Bring the needle up into the first stitch hole and work your first stitches towards the knot. When you have completed five or six, look at the reverse side of your work to check that the yarn between the knot and your stitches is held secure by the threads at the back of those stitches. If it is, turn your work over again, hold the knot firmly and away from the fabric and remove by cutting the thread with sharp scissors. If it is not secure, continue stitching until it is.

To finish off a thread, take it to the reverse side of your work and carefully thread it through the back of nearby stitches.

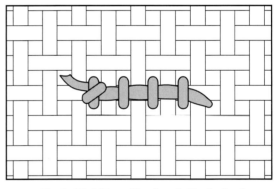

Fig 1 Finishing off a thread (the back of the fabric is shown)

FOLLOWING A CHART

The stitch charts are black and white symbol charts. Each square represents either a ‘square’ of Aida fabric or two threads of linen (or evenweave), unless otherwise indicated. Each of the symbols represents a different colour thread and a key is provided alongside the charted design.

THE STITCHES

Cross Stitch

There are several ways of working cross stitch, but the one I prefer is to make each stitch one by one (A), rather than working with a series of half-crosses and then doubling back to make full crosses (B). I find that this method reduces the chance of distorting the fabric. Whichever method you use, ensure that all your top diagonals are worked in the same direction.

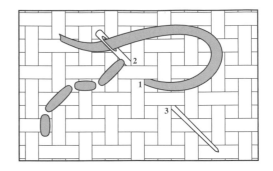

Fig 3 Working back stitch.

Straight Stitch

The length of each straight stitch can vary according to the width or length of the area to be filled in but should not be too long or loose.

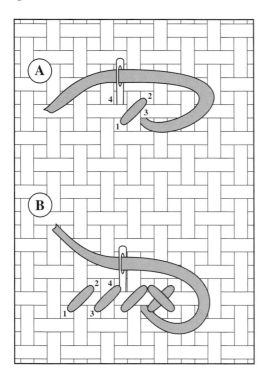

Fig 2 Working a full cross stitch.

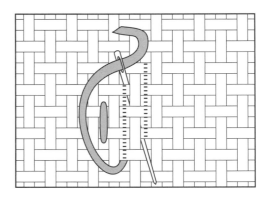

Fig 4 By varying the length of the straight stitches a shaped motif can be formed.

Half Cross Stitch

This is simply half a cross stitch. It may be worked from right to left or vice versa.

Back Stitch

This is used for some of the smaller detailed areas and occasionally for outlining (which should always be worked *after* the cross stitch it is outlining). It is also the basis for the shapes in the blackwork in the Edwardian Silhouette Picture. Back stitch may be worked diagonally, vertically or horizontally.

Padded Straight Stitch

The surface layer of this stitch is worked as shown above. However, for a three-dimensional look the stitch is lined with straight

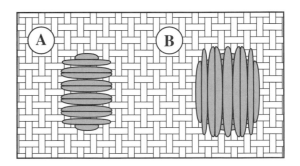

Fig 5 Padded straight stitch produces three-dimensional motifs in your embroidery

stitch worked at right angles to the top layer's desired direction. The first (padding) stitches (A) are worked slightly inside the edges of the outline of the shape, to give the top layer a rounded effect (B).

French Knots

The secret of successful French knots is to keep the piece of thread between the fabric and that held in your hand as taut as possible. Bring the needle through to the fabric front. Hold the thread about 1½in (4cm) from the fabric. Wrap the thread round the needle. Keeping the yarn between your fingers taut, place the needle where you wish to make the knot. Slowly take the needle to the back of the fabric, releasing the taut thread gradually.

Fig 6   Working a French knot.

Double Cross Stitch

To form a double cross stitch work a cross stitch first, then add a vertical cross on top. It is important to remember to ensure that the top diagonal of each cross stitch is worked in the same direction.

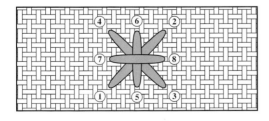

Fig 7   Double cross stitch.

Stitching Mock Tassels

Mock tassels are an effective addition to cross stitch, as seen in the Arabian Camels. Stitch the tassel head by working a series of short straight stitches between two sets of two holes; work the strands of the tassel starting at the bottom of the tassel head. Splay out the bottom strands to imitate a tassel.

Fig 8   Working a mock tassel.

Multi-coloured mock tassels adorn the harnesses of the Arabian Camels (see page 85).

EDWARDIAN SILHOUETTE PICTURE

Silhouettes make the most elegant pictures and this simple composition is enhanced by being decorated with a blackwork border and landscape. The small stencil must be cut out carefully but the spraying itself is very simple. For a slightly different effect you could omit the border pattern and add a mount instead.

FINISHED SIZE framed 6¼ × 7½in (16 × 19cm)

MATERIALS

- ◆ One copy of the silhouette pattern photocopied onto A4 card
- ◆ 28 count Zweigart Linen, in either Ivory or White, 10 × 12in (25 × 30cm)
- ◆ Spray paint in Black
- ◆ Spray Mount adhesive
- ◆ Sharp small-bladed scissors
- ◆ Embroidery frame
- ◆ Backing board for mounting work
- ◆ Narrow black picture frame, outer measurement 6¼ × 7½in (16 × 19cm)
- ◆ DMC stranded embroidery cotton (floss), 310 Black, 934 Dark Green, 732 Dark Moss, 734 Golden Moss, 3013 Pale Sage, 522 Silver Green, 3817 Turquoise and 988 Green

PREPARATION AND SPRAYING

1. Prepare the linen for work by ironing out any creases and laying the fabric on a firm flat surface.

2. Carefully cut out the black areas of the silhouette pattern with sharp, small-bladed scissors.

3. Spray the reverse side of the stencil with a thin coat of Spray Mount adhesive and position it onto the centre of the fabric. (The bottom of the man's right shoe should be horizontally level.) Adjust as required then press the stencil firmly onto the fabric.

4. Spray with a light coat of Black paint. Check that you have covered all the cut-out area with paint then remove the stencil.

STITCHING

All the stitching is worked using single strands of embroidery thread. Place the linen in a frame and work the woman's skirt in the position shown. Next work the landscape and finish with the blackwork border pattern.

EDWARDIAN SILHOUETTE STENCIL
Photocopy same size

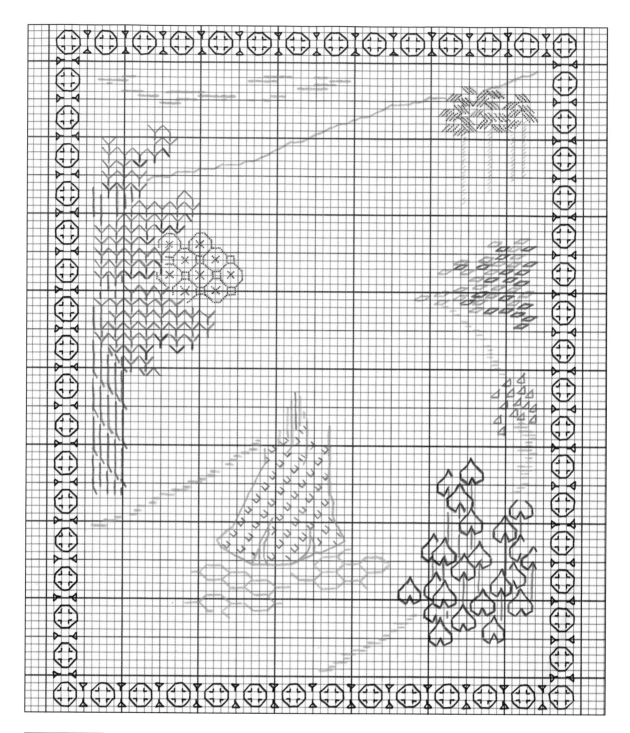

X	310
X	934
X	732
X	734
X	3013
X	522
X	3817
X	988

MAKING UP AND FINISHING

Remove any creases created by the frame, taking care not to iron the sprayed areas. Attach your stitched piece to the backing board by the method you prefer (see page 126). To complete, place the mounted work in your chosen frame.

DELFT TILE WALL HANGING

A simple masking technique using double-sided adhesive tape is used for this wall hanging. The inspiration for this piece is a set of early Dutch tiles. Their appeal is a combination of subtle colours and the tranquil scenery. The completed design makes a decorative addition to either a country-style kitchen or an entrance hall. You can also use the tiles for either a four-tile square cushion or a six-tile rectangular cushion by repeating one or more of the motifs. Alternatively, stitch one tile only to make a framed picture (see page 26).

FINISHED SIZE 5¼ × 15¾in (13.5 × 40cm)

MATERIALS

- 14 count Zweigart Aida in White, 7¾ × 22in (20 × 56cm)
- Spray paint in Royal Blue
- Thin card, 5in (12.75cm) square
- Double-sided adhesive tape
- Masking tape and scrap card
- Tapestry frame
- Iron-on hemming tape, 1½yd (1½m)
- Pair of Framecraft wooden bell-pull ends
- Hanging cord, 1yd (1m)
- Three tassels to match cord
- DMC stranded embroidery cotton (floss), 921 Terra Cotta, 725 Gold, 3822 Pale Gold, 989 Green, 367 Dark Green, 798 Dark Blue, 3753 Pale Blue and 3041 Taupe

PREPARATION AND SPRAYING

1. Take strips of double-sided adhesive tape 6in (15cm) long and cut them lengthways into further strips so that each strip measures 6in (15cm) long by two stitches of the Aida wide. You will need ten strips to represent the grouted areas. (There is no need to cut the edges of the strips exactly straight because the age and hand-made nature of the tiles mean that the line between the pattern and the grouting is often imprecise.)

2. Prepare the Aida by removing any creases and laying the fabric on a flat surface. Place the square piece of thin card in the centre of the fabric so that the edges line up with the rows of holes in the Aida.

3. Surround the edges of the card with four narrow strips of tape. Make sure the strips cover two rows of the fabric and overlap the ends of the tape where they meet.

4. Move the template to create the next tile alongside the first. With the first strips acting as a guide, place three more strips for grouting round the square template. Create the third tile in the same way alongside the centre tile.

5. Remove the template and place scrap card, secured with masking tape, round the outer edges of the piece, attaching it to the top, bottom and long side edges of the group of tiles.

6. Spray Royal Blue *lightly* along each of the strips of narrow tape in turn so that the paint falls in areas up to and parallel with the narrow grouting strips (see photograph on page 24). Then carefully remove the masking strips and scrap card.

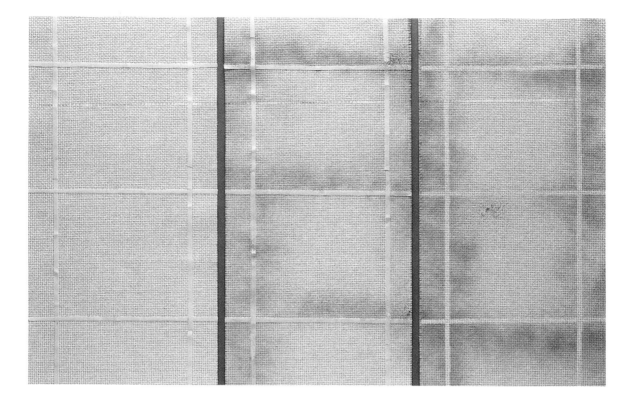

To create the grouted tile effect the background fabric is masked off with narrow strips of tape and the paint is sprayed along the edges of the tape.

STITCHING

All the stitching is worked using two strands of embroidery cotton (floss).

1. Mount the Aida onto a tapestry frame. Stitch each tile design in turn, commencing at the top with tile A (page 26).

2. Remove from the frame and lie the Aida flat, placing a magazine at each end to reverse the curling created by the frame.

MAKING UP AND FINISHING

1. Finish the side edges by trimming the Aida to the width of the iron-on hemming tape plus two stitches width of the Aida.

2. Turn the side edges to the back to leave a two-stitch-wide margin at the front of the design. Gently press on the reverse side of each edge down the length of the fabric, making sure the iron does not make direct contact with the sprayed areas.

3. Tuck the iron-on hemming tape into position under the side edges. Iron to secure, following the tape manufacturer's instructions.

4. At the top edge, fold the fabric so that you have two or three stitches' depth for the front and also room for the bell-pull ends.

5. Locate one bell-pull end and hold in position. Trim the Aida so that the amount of fabric on the reverse side of the design (below the bell-pull end) is equal to the width of the hemming tape. Attach the iron-on tape and slide the bell-pull end into position. Finish the bottom edge in the same way.

6. Attach the cord and tassels as shown in the photograph.

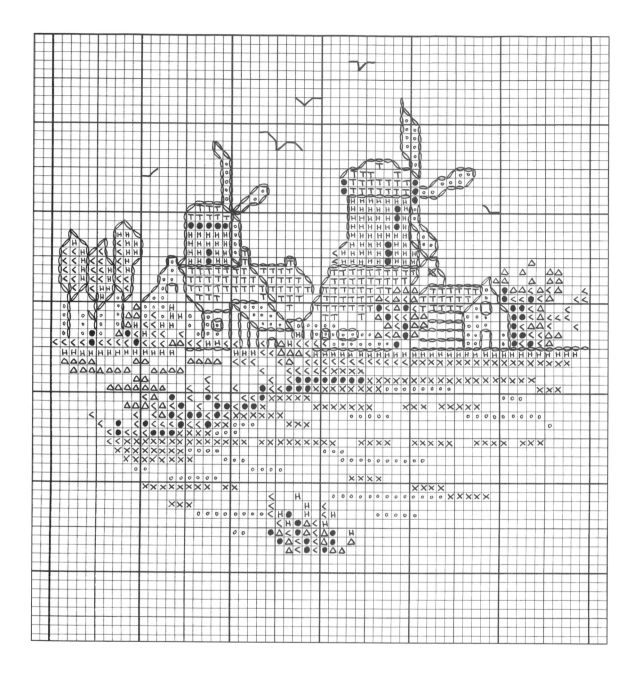

TO MAKE A FRAMED PICTURE

MATERIALS

- ♦ 14 count Zweigart Aida in White, 10in (25.5cm) square
- ♦ Spray paint in Royal Blue
- ♦ Masking tape and scrap card
- ♦ Embroidery frame (optional)
- ♦ Picture frame with inner measurement 6in (15cm) square
- ♦ DMC stranded embroidery cotton (floss) as for the Wall Hanging on page 23

TILE A

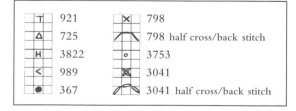

T	921	X	798
△	725	◸	798 half cross/back stitch
H	3822	○	3753
<	989	⊠	3041
●	367	◿	3041 half cross/back stitch

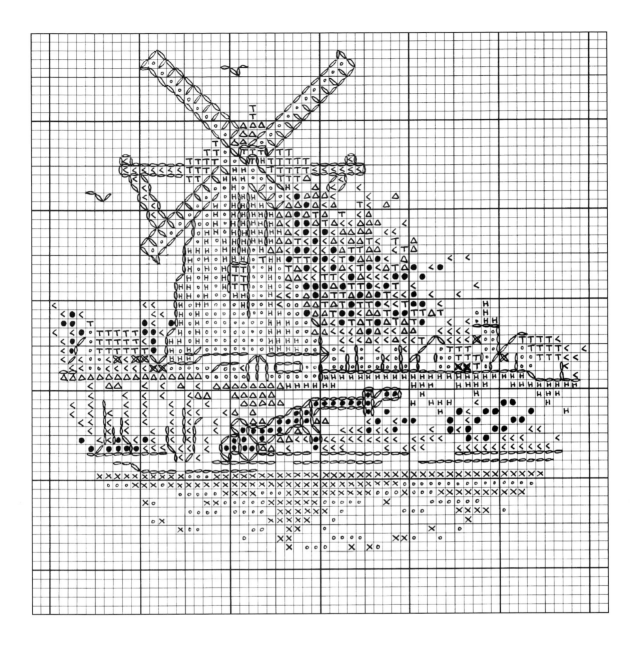

PREPARATION AND SPRAYING

1. Prepare the Aida by removing any creases and laying the fabric on a flat surface. Use masking tape to mark out a square measuring 5in (12.75cm) in the centre of the fabric. Cover the area outside the square with masking tape and scrap card.

2. Spray Royal Blue *lightly* along each of the four edges of the exposed square. Carefully remove all the masking tape and card.

TILE B

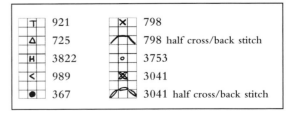

T	921	X	798	
△	725	╱╲	798 half cross/back stitch	
H	3822	o	3753	
<	989	⊠	3041	
●	367	╱╲	3041 half cross/back stitch	

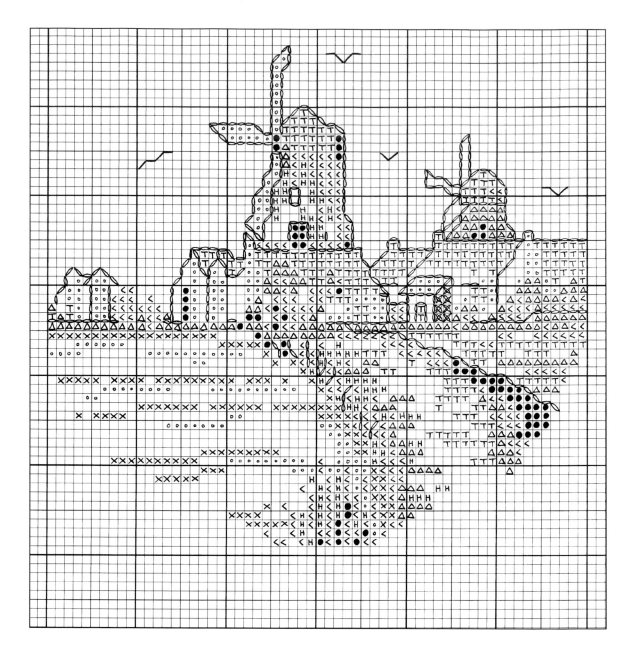

STITCHING

1. Place the Aida in the embroidery frame if using one. Stitch tile design B. Add a backstitch border to emphasize the tile edges using a single strand of 3753 Pale Blue.

MAKING UP AND FINISHING

Refer to the Flowering Bonsai Pictures (page 49) for framing information.

TILE C

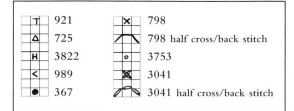

T	921	✕	798
△	725	◸	798 half cross/back stitch
H	3822	o	3753
<	989	⊠	3041
●	367	◿	3041 half cross/back stitch

ROSE TRELLIS CUSHION

Roses bloom in a gorgeous range of colours and in order to create this beautiful cushion variegated yarns have been used to mimic their glory. These help to achieve shade variation and subtlety and will also encourage you to be creative. The clear plastic, adhesive-backed covering film used for masking makes it easy to construct the basic trellis pattern.

FINISHED SIZE   14½in (37cm) square

MATERIALS

- Seven pieces of adhesive-backed clear covering film, each 4in (10cm) square
- 14 count Zweigart Aida in White, 18in (45.5cm) square
- Spray paint in Jasmine Yellow
- Tapestry frame
- Backing fabric for cushion, approximately 16in (41cm) square
- Sewing thread to match
- Cushion pad
- Piping cord, 2½yd (2¼m)
- DMC stranded embroidery cotton (floss), 987 Holly Green, 989 Medium Green, 3348 Apple Green, 436 Tobacco, 51 Variegated Orange, 106 Variegated Orange Pink, 57 Variegated Dark Pink, 48 Variegated Medium Pink and 62 Variegated Pale Pink

PREPARATION AND SPRAYING

1. Cut two of the pieces of adhesive-backed clear covering film in half diagonally to create four triangular pieces.

2. Remove the backing paper from one of the squares of adhesive-backed film and place in the centre of the Aida to create a central diamond. Make sure the edges of the film exactly match a diagonal line of holes in the Aida. Re-position if necessary to achieve this.

3. Following the positions shown in the photograph, and working outwards, place the other squares and then the triangular pieces

onto the Aida. Leave six holes, counting diagonally (twelve holes on the horizontal), between each piece of film. This will create diagonal strips twelve holes wide.

4. Spray the whole piece with enough light sprayings of Jasmine Yellow to produce a solid covering. Finally, remove the pieces of film.

The green felt pieces in this photograph show you how to position the pieces of adhesive-backed clear covering film onto the fabric to create a trellis pattern once sprayed.

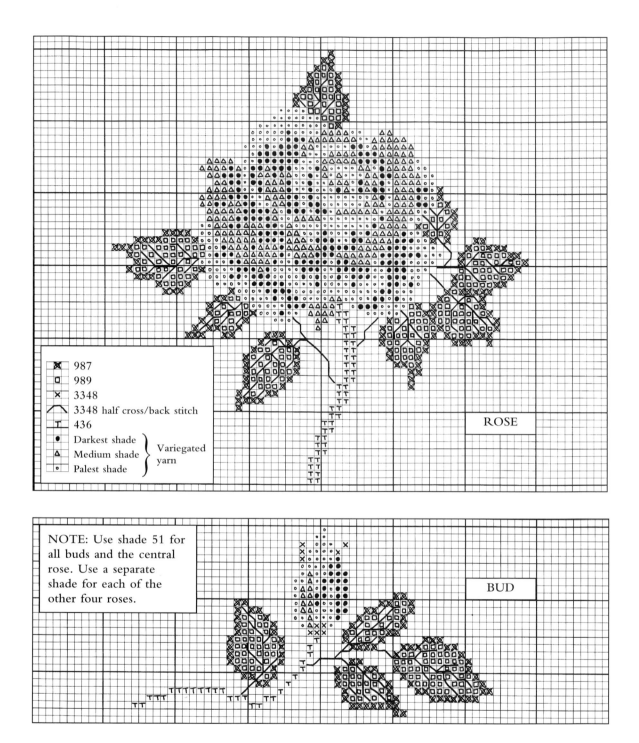

Key:

Symbol	Shade
☒	987
▫	989
✕	3348
⌒	3348 half cross/back stitch
⊤	436
●	Darkest shade
△	Medium shade
▫	Palest shade

} Variegated yarn

ROSE

NOTE: Use shade 51 for all buds and the central rose. Use a separate shade for each of the other four roses.

BUD

STITCHING

All the stitching is worked using three strands of embroidery cotton (floss). Mount the Aida onto a tapestry frame and work each rose and bud motif in turn, commencing at the top and working downwards.

MAKING UP AND FINISHING

1. Remove from the frame. Trim the Aida, leaving ⅝in (1.5cm) seam allowance. Place the right sides of the Aida and backing fabric together, using tacking (basting) stitches to secure the two. Then machine stitch the top and two sides.

2. Remove the tacking (basting) from the bottom edge and turn right side out. Then press the seam allowance on the bottom edge, insert the cushion pad and close up with oversewing, leaving a small opening for tucking in the ends of the piping cord.

The Rose Trellis Cushion and Nasturtium Herb Pillow (see page 32 for instructions).

3. To finish, attach the cord with neat hand stitching.

NASTURTIUM HERB PILLOW

This pretty herb pillow makes a colourful addition to a guest room or a favourite chair.
The bottom edge is fastened with ribbon so the herbs can be refreshed with ease. If you wish to use it as a
cushion you can omit the herbs and ribbon and close up the bottom edge. The spray painting allows you to
complete the cushion (or even a pair) in fine Aida in a very short space of time.

FINISHED SIZE 13 × 11in (33 × 28cm)

MATERIALS

- One copy of the leaves outline photocopied onto A3 card
- One copy of the diamonds and flowers outline photocopied onto A3 card
- 18 count Zweigart Aida in White, 18 × 16in (45.5 × 41cm)
- Spray paints in Sunburst Red, Orange, Jasmine Yellow, Parrot Green and Leaf Green
- Spray Mount adhesive
- Scrap card
- Masking tape
- Tapestry frame
- Backing fabric for the cushion, 14½ × 12½in (37 × 32cm)
- Piece of thick wadding (trimmed to fit the pillow but twice its height)
- Ribbon for fastening, approximately 1⅔yd (1½m)

- Herbs or pot-pourri mix
- DMC stranded embroidery cotton (floss), 470 Green, 472 Lime Green, 745 Pale Yellow, 972 Dark Yellow, 741 Pale Orange, 608 Dark Orange, 351 Pinky Red and 349 Red

PREPARATION AND SPRAYING

1. Cut out the stencils.

2. Apply Spray Mount adhesive to the reverse side of the leaf stencil. Remove any creases from the Aida and place on a flat surface. Place the stencil in the centre of the Aida.

The spraying of the fabric is a two-stage process. First apply and spray the leaf stencil, then the diamonds and flower stencil as described in steps 3–6 on page 34.

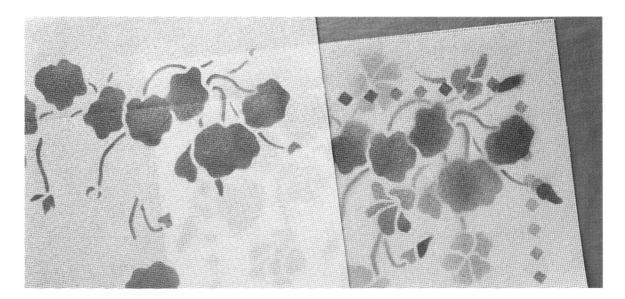

NASTURTIUM STENCIL Enlarge to 140%

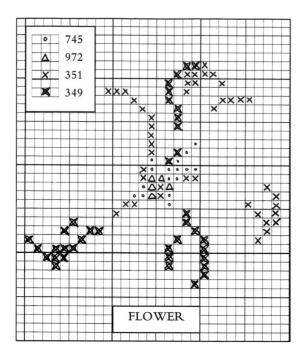

◦	745
△	972
✕	351
✖	349

FLOWER

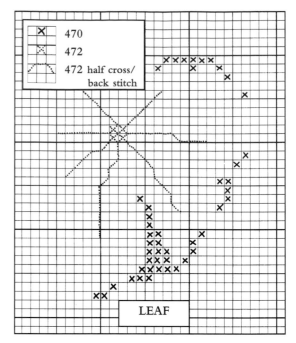

✕	470
⋰	472
⌢	472 half cross/ back stitch

LEAF

3. Cover all areas outside the stencil with scrap card and masking tape then spray the stencil with Parrot Green.

4. Add Leaf Green to the outer edges of the larger leaves and then remove the stencil and scrap card.

5. Apply Spray Mount adhesive to the reverse side of the diamonds and flower stencil and place it on the Aida so that it links up with, but does not overlap, the sprayed leaves. Replace the scrap card and masking tape.

6. Spray the flowers and diamonds in turn, choosing from Sunburst Red, Orange and Jasmine Yellow in a combination of your choice. Remove the stencil and scrap card.

STITCHING

All the stitching is worked using two strands of embroidery cotton (floss).

1. Attach the Aida to the tapestry frame, then begin stitching by working the leaves using the chart as a guide, varying the length of the vein lines according to the size of the leaf.

2. Work the nasturtium flowers using the chart as a guide. You can vary the colours used as appropriate (refer to the Materials list on page 32 for a suggested thread palette).

MAKING UP AND FINISHING

1. Follow steps 1–3 in the Making Up and Finishing instructions for the Rose Trellis Cushion on page 30, but do not insert a pad, and hem the bottom edges rather than close them up.

2. Neatly attach four pieces of ribbon to the bottom edge of the cushion.

3. Sprinkle the herbs or pot-pourri mix onto the centre of the wadding and fold it in half, placing it inside the cushion so that the fold is at the bottom edge of the cushion, to prevent the herbs falling out.

4. Tie the ribbons to neatly close up the bottom edge.

LODGE DOOR BOOK COVER

This design can be used to cover various kinds of book. The one in the photograph has been used to cover an A5 file that is used as a gardening diary and which houses notes on pruning, cultivation, garden plans and plant lists. It is useful to have all this information in one place under such a suitably attractive cover.

FINISHED SIZE to fit a book 7 × 9in (18 × 23cm)

MATERIALS

- Two copies of the door pattern photocopied onto A4 card
- 14 count Zweigart Aida Rustico, 19 x 12½in (48 × 32cm)
- Spray paints in Tuscan Beige and Leaf Green
- Masking tape
- Scrap card
- Tapestry frame
- Double-sided adhesive tape
- Book blank to cover, 7 × 9in (18 × 23cm)
- DMC stranded embroidery cotton (floss), 613 Stone, 640 Dark Stone, 350 Brick Red, 3706 Pink, 3716 Pale Pink, 602 Pale Fuchsia, 102 Variegated Purple, 126 Variegated Lilac, 340 Pale Bluebell, 472 Lime Green, 471 Green, 988 Medium Green and 413 Dark Grey

PREPARATION AND SPRAYING

1. From one copy of the door pattern cut out the cream-coloured door area. From the other, cut out all the solid black lines.

2. Remove any creases from the Aida and fold the fabric in half to create the shape of the finished book cover. Place a piece of scrap card between the two halves of the fabric (to avoid paint seeping through the top layer of fabric onto the inside book cover).

3. Place the door stencil in the centre of the folded fabric widthways and just above the centre. (The bottom edge of the door should be approximately 3½in (9cm) above the bottom edge of the front cover. The door bottom edge and sides should line up with the holes of the Aida.)

The photograph below shows how your fabric should look once both stencils have been sprayed as directed in steps 4 and 5 on page 39.

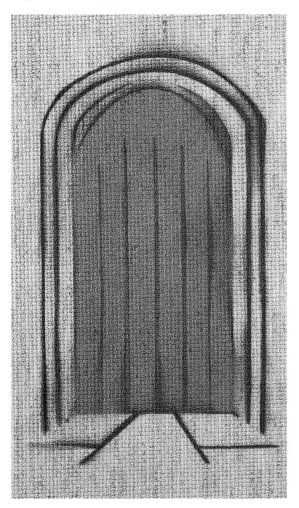

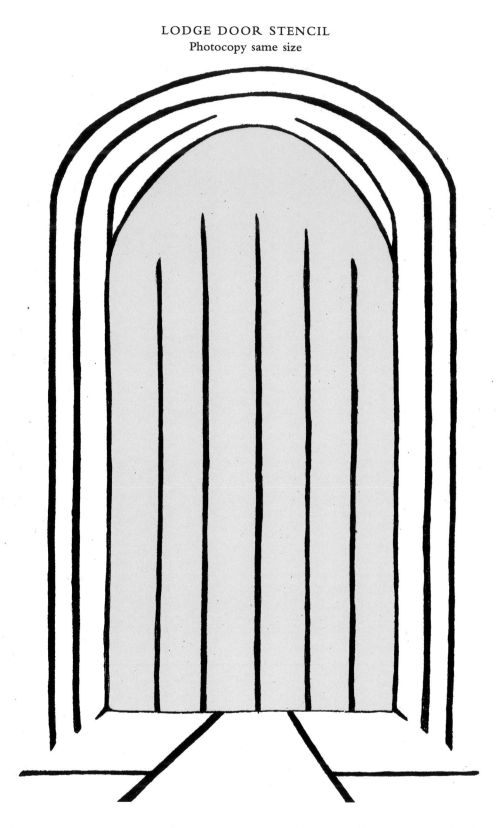

Note: As the stencils are used without Spray Mount adhesive it is important to direct your spraying of the second stencil in such a way that paint does not drift too much under the stencil. Therefore direct your spray by holding the can parallel to the fabric.

LEFT-HAND CONTAINER

⊠	613
╱	613 half cross/back stitch
⚹	640
╱	640 half cross/back stitch
⦰	350
✳	3706
╱	3706 half cross/back stitch
•	3716
△	602
■	102
╱	102 half cross/back stitch
▢	126
S	340
L	472
⌢	472 half cross/back stitch
✛	471
▼	988
⊠	413
╱	413 half cross/back stitch

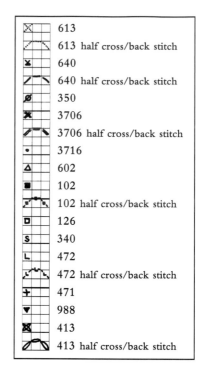

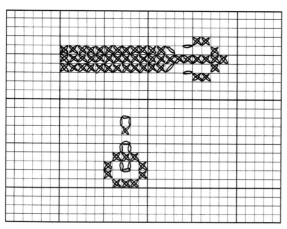

DOOR FURNITURE
Note: door hinges are stitched twice

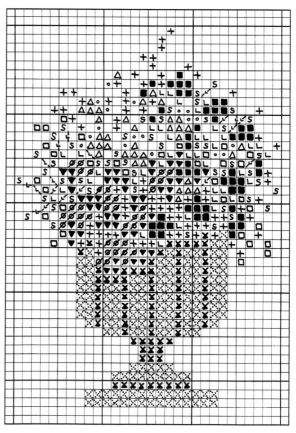

RIGHT-HAND CONTAINER

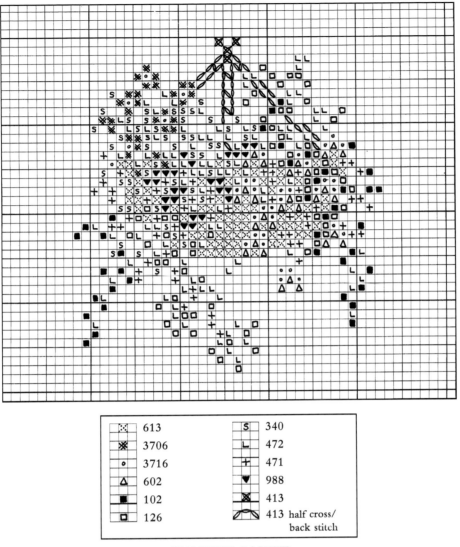

⬚	613	S	340
✳	3706	L	472
∘	3716	+	471
△	602	▼	988
■	102	✕	413
⬛	126	⟋	413 half cross/ back stitch

HANGING BASKET

4. Mask any Aida showing outside the stencil, then spray a solid covering of Tuscan Beige.

5. Remove the door stencil and position the second stencil so that it lines up with the sprayed area. Re-apply masking to the area outside the stencil. Spray first with Tuscan Beige, then Leaf Green.

STITCHING

All the stitching is worked using two strands of embroidery cotton (floss). Work the hanging basket chart, making sure that the centre of the top of the basket chain is midway across the door width. Stitch the door furniture then the two container charts.

MAKING UP AND FINISHING

1. Fold the fabric so that it covers the book or file appropriately.

2. Use double-sided adhesive tape to secure the Aida to the insides of the book cover, then trim off any excess fabric.

STRIPED PICTURE FRAME

This is a very unusual way of creating a frame for photographs and the cut-out frame middle can be used to either create a second smaller frame or the paperweight illustrated. Either separately or together they make an ideal inexpensive gift for a friend or relative. The use of Aida Plus means that no embroidery frame is needed.

FINISHED SIZE frame according to size of your photograph; paperweight approximately 3in (7.5cm) in diameter

MATERIALS

- One A4 sheet of thick card (for small frame as illustrated; use A3 for a larger frame)
- One sheet of Zweigart Aida Plus in Ivory (makes two frames of the size shown)
- Spray paints in Jasmine Yellow, Highland Green, Royal Blue and Leaf Green
- Double-sided adhesive tape
- Medium-thick string
- One A4 sheet of mount board
- DMC paperweight blank (if required)
- DMC stranded embroidery cotton (floss), 550 Dark Purple, 3746 Mauve, 988 Green, 986 Dark Green, 743 Yellow and 726 Lemon

PREPARATION AND SPRAYING

1. Mark clearly at the edge of the thick card ⁵⁄₁₀in (1.5cm) intervals along all four sides. Attach double-sided adhesive tape to all the front edges of the card.

2. Cut the Aida Plus in half and locate one piece in the centre of the thick card. (If making a large frame, place the whole sheet of Aida Plus in the centre of an A3 sheet of thick card.)

3. Beginning in the top left-hand corner, place lengths of string cut to the appropriate sizes diagonally across the Aida Plus, from mark to mark as shown in the photograph. The double-sided adhesive tape will keep the string in position.

4. Using horizontal bands of colour coverage, spray the fabric with the four paint colours in more or less equal bands over the fabric. (If desired you can substitute a different set of colours to match your own photograph.) Carefully remove enough of the string to enable you to slide out the fabric.

5. To make another frame, slide in another piece of Aida Plus under the remaining strings and replace those pieces of string removed. Spray again. Repeat as required.

The photograph below shows how string has been used to mask areas on the fabric to produce the striped effect.

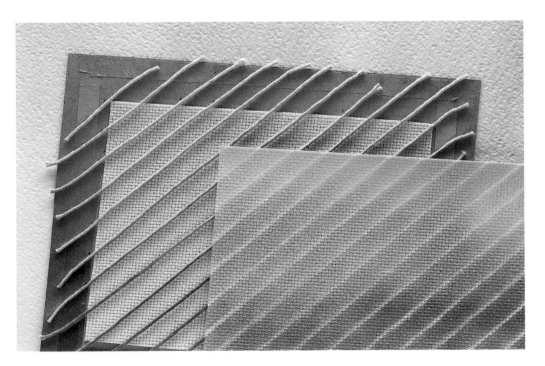

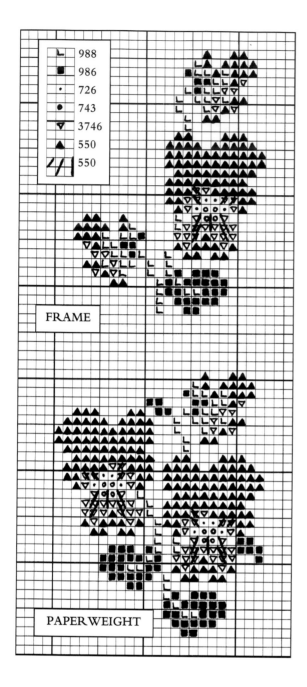

⌐	988
■	986
·	726
●	743
▽	3746
▲	550
▧	550

FRAME

PAPERWEIGHT

MAKING UP AND FINISHING

1. Cut out the centre of the frame by measuring the photograph and subtracting ⅜in (1cm) from each dimension to calculate the size of the area to be cut. Begin cutting near the motif and try to cut out the central area in one piece if you want to make the matching paperweight.

2. Carefully trim the outer edges of the Aida Plus so that the frame is a consistent width all round. Attach double-sided adhesive tape to the bottom and the two side edges of the reverse side of your frame, leaving a ⅛in (5mm) gap between the inner edge of the frame and the tape. Place the frame onto the mount board and press firmly to secure the two pieces together. Carefully trim the mount board to the size of the frame.

3. Use the mount board trimmings to create a back-prop support. This needs to be scored lightly with a craft knife approximately ¾in (2cm) from the top to allow it to bend. Attach this to the reverse side of the mount board using double-sided adhesive tape. Slide your photograph into the frame via the unstuck top edge.

TO MAKE THE PAPERWEIGHT

Use the spray painted fabric cut out from the centre of the frame to make the complementary paperweight.

1. Work the pansy motif in the centre of the remaining fabric following the chart shown on this page.

2. To finish the paperweight, trim the stitched Aida Plus to the size of the paperweight blank's inner rim. Place in position and attach the self-adhesive backing supplied with the paperweight blank.

STITCHING

All stitching is worked using two strands of embroidery cotton (floss). Locate your photograph in the centre of the Aida Plus so that you can determine the right position to start stitching the pansy motif, then work the design.

QUICK AND EASY
CHRISTMAS CARDS

Stitching enthusiasts would occasionally like to be able to produce a series of Christmas cards but usually only complete a few to send to close family members. With this set of stencils you can produce a whole collection in a few evenings. The Christmas tree card is a good way of using up all those odd lengths of thread and the candle card can be sprayed any colour to ring the changes.

FINISHED SIZE OF CARD   4¼ × 6⅛in
(11 × 15.5cm)

MATERIALS
- Chosen design(s) photocopied onto card (two copies of the Robin needed)
- For each design a piece of 18 count Zweigart Aida in Ivory or Cream, 4 × 6in (10 × 15cm)
- Spray paints as follows: Sunburst Red and Highland Green for the Tree; Sunburst Red, Highland Green, Brown and Black for the Robin; Yellow, Highland Green and chosen candle colour(s) for the Candle and Ivy
- Spray Mount adhesive
- Masking tape
- Double-sided adhesive tape
- Suitable DMC card blanks with matching envelopes (choose a colour to complement the design and your threads)
- DMC metallic thread in gold
- DMC stranded embroidery cotton (floss), 3347 Leaf Green, 3348 Apple Green, 727 Lemon, 721 Orange and 606 Scarlet (plus oddments of suitable colours)

TREE STENCIL

CANDLE AND IVY STENCIL
Photocopy all stencils same size

ROBIN STENCIL

PREPARATION AND SPRAYING

THE TREE

1. Cut out the tree tub from the stencil and place the card onto the Aida.

2. Spray the tree tub with Red paint, then remove the stencil.

3. Cut out the tree from the stencil and spray the back with Spray Mount adhesive. Relocate onto the Aida, lining up the tree tub.

4. Cover the tree tub area with a small piece of masking tape and spray the tree Green. (You can vary the green, as illustrated in the photograph opposite.) Remove the stencil.
Note: If you wish to produce several cards, spray all the tree tubs before cutting out the tree.

The spraying of the fabric for the Robin card is a two-stage process. Carefully position the second stencil as described in step 4.

THE ROBIN

1. Cut out the face/chest area from one piece of photocopied card and all the other areas from the second piece.

2. Apply Spray Mount adhesive to the reverse side of each stencil.

3. Place the face/chest stencil onto the fabric and spray with Red paint. Remove this stencil.

4. Position the second stencil so that the head area meets the robin's face without overlapping or leaving any gaps. Spray the body and head with Brown paint. Now apply small amounts of Black paint to the eye, beak and feet areas. (You can shield the brown areas with masking tape, provided of course you leave space in the tape for the Black paint.)

5. Spray the leaves Green then remove the stencil. (If you prefer, use more than one shade of green for the leaves.)

THE CANDLE AND IVY

1. Cut out the candle and flame areas from the stencil and place onto the fabric.

2. Spray the flame with Yellow paint and the candle your chosen colour.

3. Remove the stencil, cover the candle and flame with masking tape and cut out the ivy.

4. Spray the reverse side of the stencil with Spray Mount adhesive and relocate onto the Aida.

5. Spray with Green paint then remove the stencil.

Note: As with the tree design, spray all your candles and flames first if producing several cards, before cutting out the area to be sprayed green.

STITCHING

Work the chart(s) for your chosen design(s) using two strands of embroidery cotton (floss) for all stitches. Use the gold thread as it comes from the reel but use two lengths on the needle.

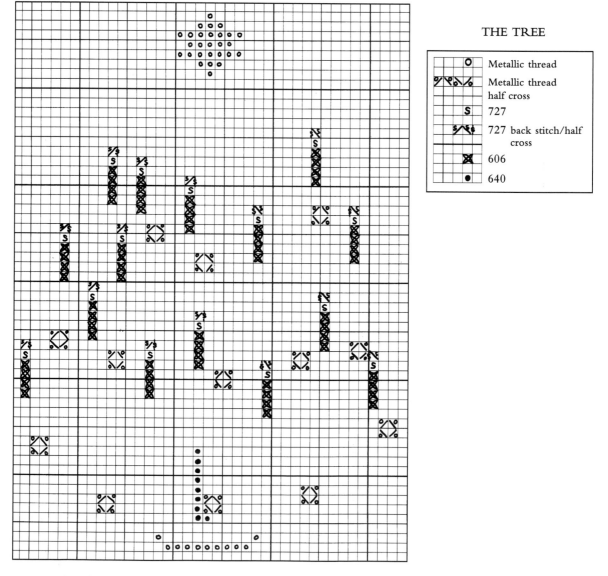

THE TREE

O	Metallic thread
	Metallic thread half cross
S	727
	727 back stitch/half cross
✕	606
●	640

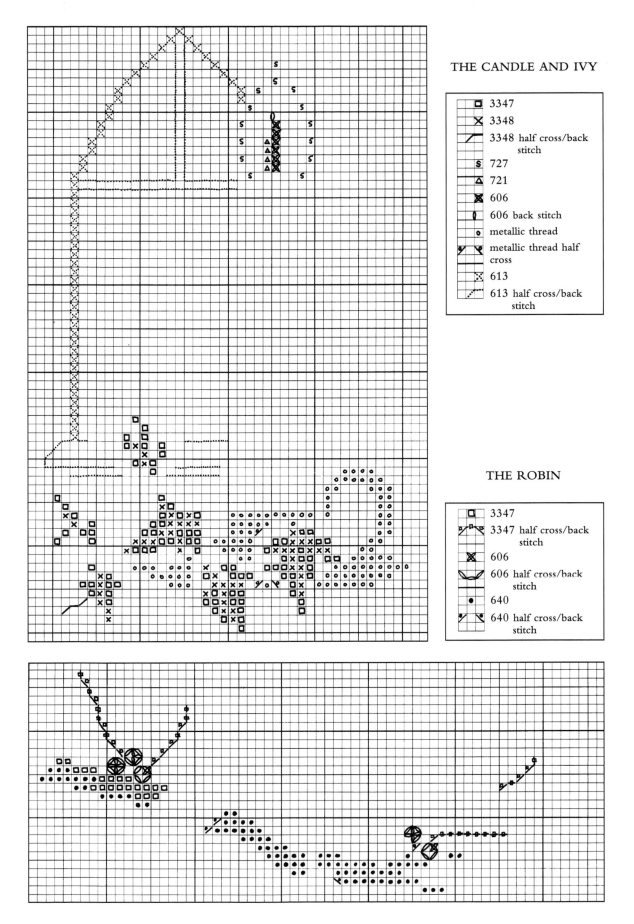

THE CANDLE AND IVY

	3347
X	3348
/	3348 half cross/back stitch
s	727
△	721
✕	606
◖	606 back stitch
o	metallic thread
⬦ ⬥	metallic thread half cross
▨	613
⋰	613 half cross/back stitch

THE ROBIN

	3347
▷ ◁	3347 half cross/back stitch
X	606
◣	606 half cross/back stitch
•	640
◢ ◣	640 half cross/back stitch

MAKING UP AND FINISHING

1. To mount your work in a card, first open up the card and attach strips of double-sided adhesive tape to the back of the cut-out opening.

2. Position the opening over your stitched work and when it is in the correct position mark the position of the corners of the stitched work with an air-soluble pen. (Lines of the fabric weave should be parallel to the edges of the opening.) Also mark the fabric where it overlaps the edges of the card.

3. Cut away any excess material, cutting just inside any lines made with the air-soluble pen.

4. Remove the protective strip from the double-sided tape and locate the stitched work in the correct position, matching the corner marks with the corner edges. Press the card and fabric firmly.

5. Place a strip of double-sided adhesive tape on the back of the needlework, along the edge required to secure the part of the card which will act as a backing to the needlework.

6. Take a piece of paper slightly smaller than twice the size of the front of the card. Crease the paper down the centre. Open out the card and paper and remove the protective strip from the adhesive tape. Attach the paper to the reverse side of the needlework, lining up the creases.

7. Place a strip of double-sided adhesive tape down the inside of the piece of card which will secure the reverse side of the needlework. Remove the protective strip and press the backing card firmly. Your needlework will now be completely secure, as will its backing cover, and you can use the paper to write your message on. Rather than use white paper for the insert, choose cream for a sophisticated finish.

By choosing an alternative colour for the candle, the Candle and Ivy design makes an attractive Easter card.

FLOWERING BONSAI PICTURES

Bonsai trees are a way of enjoying some of the benefits and pleasures of gardening, even if your home is without a patch of soil. They are surprisingly easy to maintain and give years of pleasure but, if you prefer to see bonsai in bloom all the year round, why not stitch this pair of pictures to brighten up your walls? Some of the materials are listed separately but the instructions apply to both designs.

FINISHED SIZE framed 10¼ × 12¼in (26 × 31cm)

MATERIALS

- One copy of Wisteria or Crab Apple tree trunk pattern photocopied onto A4 card
- 14 count Zweigart Aida in Cream (for the Crab Apple) or Antique White (for the Wisteria), 15 × 16½in (38 × 42cm)
- Spray paints in Tuscan Beige and Leaf Green
- Spray Mount adhesive
- Tapestry frame or large embroidery frame
- Backing board for mounting needlework
- Scrap card
- Masking tape
- Double-sided adhesive tape (if covering the frame)
- Decorative paper (if covering the frame)
- Picture frame, internal size 7½ × 9½in (19 × 24cm)
- DMC Flower thread, 2732 Moss
- *For the Wisteria* DMC stranded embroidery cotton (floss), 931 Dark Air Force Blue, 926 Sea Green, 3013 Sage Green, 471 Green, 211 Pale Mauve, 554 Mauve and 553 Dark Mauve
- *For the Crab Apple* DMC stranded embroidery cotton (floss), 989 Medium Green, 3347 Leaf Green, 471 Green, 832 Dark Antique Gold, 834 Antique Gold, 726 Yellow, 746 Cream, B5200 White, 951 Flesh and 760 Blush

PREPARATION AND SPRAYING

1. Cut out the tree trunk area with sharp scissors.

2. Remove any creases from the Aida and place it on a flat surface.

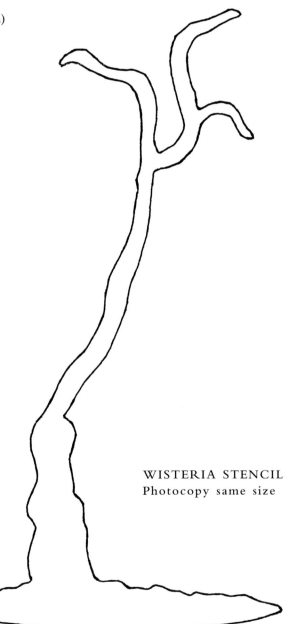

WISTERIA STENCIL
Photocopy same size

3. Spray the reverse side of the card with a thin coat of Spray Mount adhesive and position it onto the centre of the fabric.

4. Use scrap card and masking tape to protect areas of the fabric not being sprayed. Spray the whole of the trunk with Tuscan Beige paint then spray the shadow and moss along the left-hand side of the trunk using Leaf Green. Remove the stencil.

CRAB APPLE STENCIL
Photocopy same size

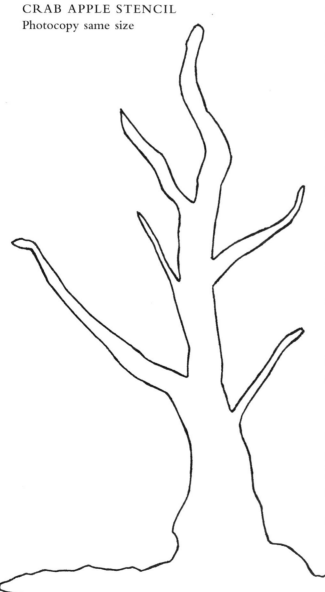

STITCHING

Place the Aida in a frame. Follow the chart of the tree of your choice (page 52/53) working from the top downwards. Use one strand of Flower thread on the trunk, two strands of embroidery cotton (floss) for the flowers and foliage and three strands for the bowl colours.

MAKING UP AND FINISHING

1. Remove any creases in the fabric taking care not to iron the sprayed areas.

2. Attach your stitched piece to the backing board by the method you prefer (see page 126). (If you are not going to cover the frame with decorative paper go straight onto final step 12.)

3. Cover the sides of the frame with double-sided adhesive tape and remove the covering.

4. Place the frame right side up on a flat surface. Position the decorative paper over it.

5. Press the paper to one of the side edges of the frame and, keeping it taut, press the paper to the opposite side edge.

6. Repeat step 5 for the other two sides.

7. Turn the frame over and attach double-sided adhesive tape to all the rebate/recess edges on the inner edge of the frame.

8. Pierce the centre of the paper and cut out a rectangular piece, leaving enough paper to cover the tape attached to the recess edges. Make a mitred (diagonal) cut towards each corner of the frame.

9. Working on each inner edge in turn, remove the protective cover on the adhesive tape and press the paper to it.

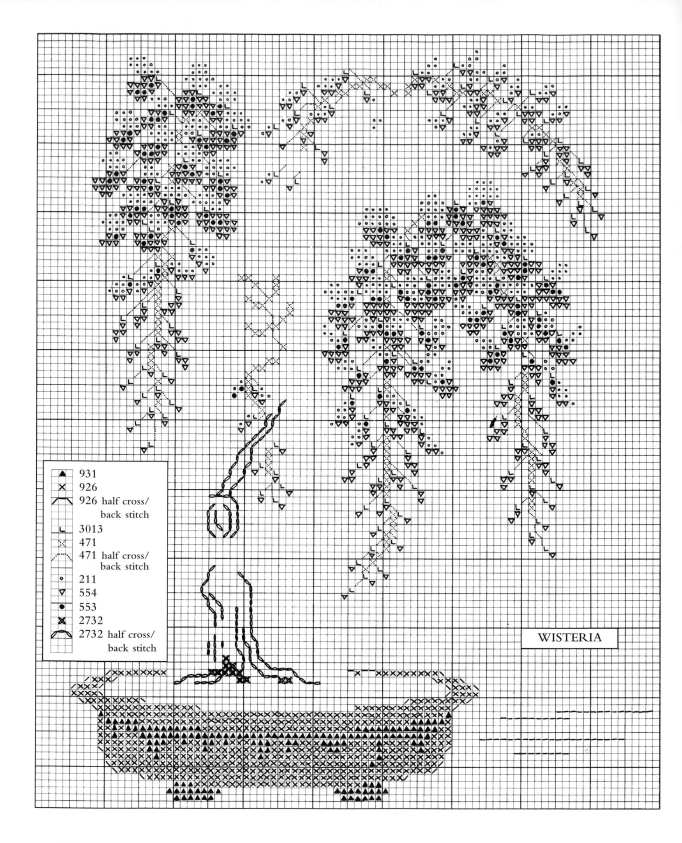

	931
	926
	926 half cross/ back stitch
	3013
	471
	471 half cross/ back stitch
	211
	554
	553
	2732
	2732 half cross/ back stitch

WISTERIA

10. Attach lengths of double-sided adhesive tape to the reverse side of the frame before removing the protective covering from the tape. Then trim the paper at the outer edges of the frame so that it completely covers the adhesive tape.

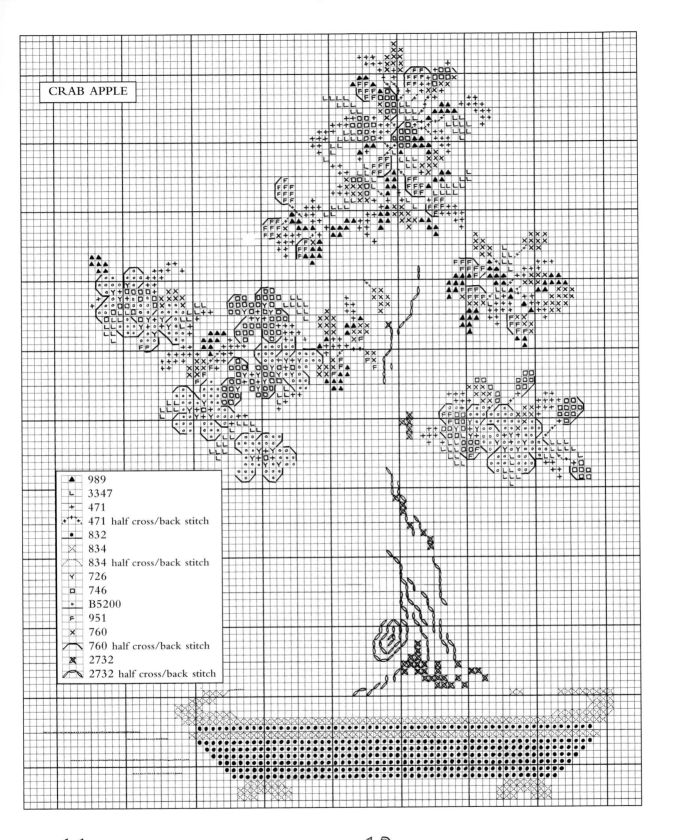

CRAB APPLE

▲	989
L	3347
+	471
+·+·+	471 half cross/back stitch
•	832
☒	834
	834 half cross/back stitch
Y	726
□	746
○	B5200
F	951
×	760
	760 half cross/back stitch
☒	2732
	2732 half cross/back stitch

11. Repeat step 9, this time working on the outer edges.

12. Place the mounted work in the frame and attach the cord and fixings.

EDWARD BEAR PEN-CASE

This delightful pen-case is very easy to make because most of the colour is created by the spraying and Velcro has been chosen as the fastening for the case to minimize any sewing and making up. It would therefore be a fun project for a child of eight years or so to make for themselves, a friend or for a younger child in the family. This pen-case would also make a suitable school project for under eleven-year olds.

FINISHED SIZE 9½ × 5¼in (24 × 13.5cm)

MATERIALS

- Two copies of the bear pattern photocopied onto A4 card
- 14 count Zweigart Aida in Ivory, 12 × 10½in (30 × 27cm)
- Spray paints in Royal Blue and Sunburst Red
- Spray Mount adhesive
- Masking tape
- Scrap card
- Ivory sewing thread
- Double-stick Velcro, 10in (25.5cm)
- DMC Medicis crewel embroidery wool, 8326 Honey and 8321 Brown
- DMC stranded embroidery cotton (floss), 310 Black, 301 Ginger and 336 Navy

PREPARATION AND SPRAYING

1. From one copy of the bear pattern cut out the jacket, and from the other copy cut out the trousers.

2. Remove any creases from the Aida and fold it in half so that it measures 6 × 10½in (15 × 27cm). Place a piece of scrap card between the two layers of Aida to avoid paint seeping through the top layer of fabric onto the inside back panel.

3. Lightly spray the reverse side of the trousers stencil with Spray Mount adhesive. Place it on the fabric so that there is a 1½in (4cm) gap between the fold edge of the Aida and the left trouser leg, and a 2in (5cm) gap

between the bottom of the trousers and the adjacent edge. (If any Aida is showing cover this up with scrap card and masking tape.)

4. Spray with Royal Blue paint and then remove the stencil. Also remove the scrap card and masking tape if this has been used, but leave in place the card protecting the inside back panel.

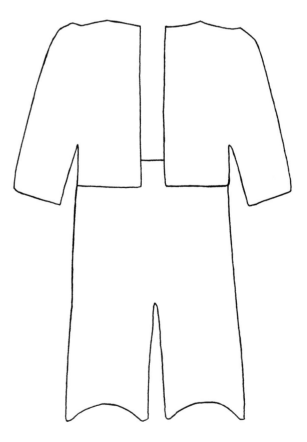

EDWARD BEAR STENCIL Enlarge to 125%

First position and spray the trouser stencil; then carefully position the jacket stencil and spray.

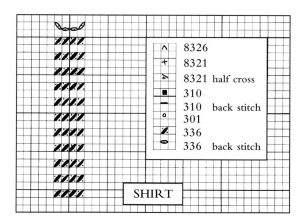

5. Lightly spray the reverse side of the jacket stencil with Spray Mount adhesive and place on the fabric so that the trousers and jacket meet but do not overlap. Use scrap card as in step 2, if required.

6. Spray with Sunburst Red paint and then remove the stencil and scrap card.

STITCHING

Work the charts for head, feet, hands and shirt using two strands of thread for all stitches.

MAKING UP AND FINISHING

1. Reverse the centre fold so that the Aida is wrong side out. Stitch both short edge seams, taking a ⅝in (1.5cm) seam allowance.

2. Turn the hem along the opening edge, using slip stitches and the same seam allowance. Turn the case so that it is right side out.

3. Remove the protective covering from the Velcro and attach to both inner edges of the case. Trim accordingly.

DOLL DRAW-STRING BAG

This bag has many potential uses and, like the previous design, it is a suitable project for a child to tackle. It could easily be adapted by changing the colour of the dress or hair to match a child's favourite doll. Although a simple design, it can be embellished to create an individualized, decorative piece.

FINISHED SIZE 9½ × 12½in (24 × 32cm)

MATERIALS

- Two copies of the doll pattern photocopied onto A4 card
- 14 count Zweigart Aida in Ivory, 20 × 15½in (51 × 39cm)
- Spray Mount adhesive
- Spray paints in Peach and Rose (or your colour(s) for dress)
- Scrap card
- Masking tape
- Tapestry frame
- Decorative beads for the cord ends
- Small amounts of narrow lace and ribbon for decorating the dress
- Ivory sewing thread
- Ivory bias binding, ¾yd (¾m)
- Cord for draw-string fastening, 1yd (1m)
- DMC stranded embroidery cotton (floss), 310 Black, 334 Blue, 472 Lime Green, 729 Dark Gold, 676 Blonde, B5200 White, 760 Blush and 3731 Dark Rose
- *Note:* You will need to change the Dark Rose if you change the dress colour. Choose a shade darker than your paint so you can stitch the shadow/creases of the dress

PREPARATION AND SPRAYING

1. From one copy of the doll pattern cut out the face, arms and legs and from the other copy cut out the dress.

2. Remove any creases from the Aida and fold in half to measure 10 × 15½in (25.5 × 39cm). Place scrap card between the two halves to avoid paint seeping through the top layer of fabric onto the inside back cover.

3. Lightly spray the back of the face and limbs stencil with Spray Mount adhesive and place on the fabric so that the bottom edges of

DOLL STENCIL Enlarge to 115%

the legs are 4in (10cm) up from the bottom edge of the bag. (The limbs should be an equal distance from each of the two side edges, allowing for the seam allowance of ⅝in (1.5cm) along the cut edges opposite the fold.) If any Aida is showing cover this up with scrap card and masking tape.

4. Use light sprayings of Peach until you achieve a flesh colour then remove the stencil.

5. Lightly spray the back of the dress stencil with Spray Mount adhesive and place on the fabric so that the dress meets the body parts.

6. Spray with Rose. Remove the stencil.

STITCHING

All the stitching is worked using two strands of embroidery thread.

1. Mount the Aida onto the tapestry frame and work the bonnet to bouquet and the socks and shoes chart on page 60.

2. Sew on the ribbon, beads and lace.

3. Work the dress skirt detail and finally the border design from the chart on page 60.

MAKING UP AND FINISHING

1. On the wrong side of the Aida, attach the bias binding 2½in (6.5cm) from the top edge across the whole width of the bag but starting and finishing 1in (2.5cm) inside the side seam edges. Leave the ends of the bias binding open so that the cord can be threaded through later.

2. Reverse the centre fold, so that the Aida is wrong side out and stitch the bottom and side

Pretty and practical – the Doll Draw-string Bag and Doily Cushion (page 61).

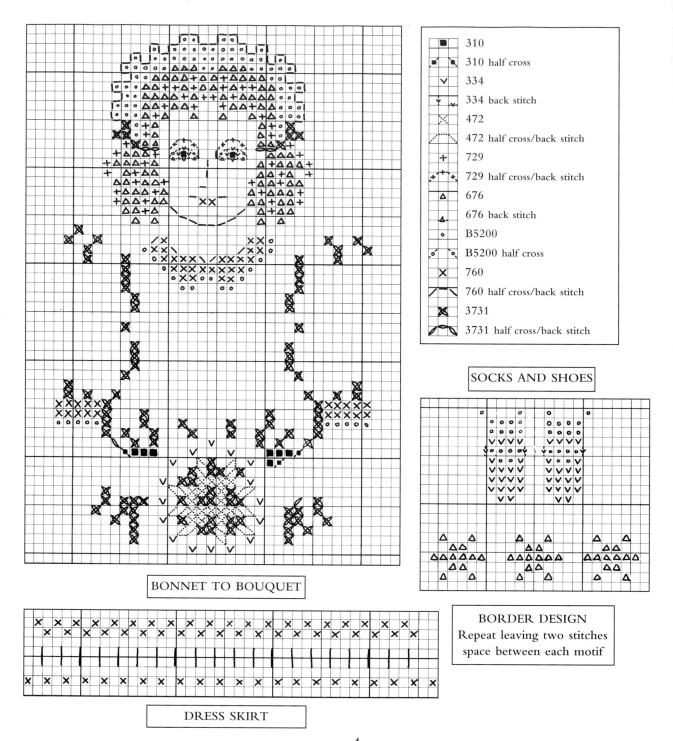

	310
	310 half cross
V	334
	334 back stitch
	472
	472 half cross/back stitch
+	729
	729 half cross/back stitch
△	676
	676 back stitch
○	B5200
	B5200 half cross
X	760
	760 half cross/back stitch
X	3731
	3731 half cross/back stitch

SOCKS AND SHOES

BONNET TO BOUQUET

BORDER DESIGN
Repeat leaving two stitches
space between each motif

DRESS SKIRT

edge seams, taking a ⅝in (1.5cm) seam allowance but leaving a gap where the bias binding starts and finishes.

3. Fold the top edge under and press a ¼in (6mm) hem allowance. Fold again and slipstitch the top edge hem to the stitching of the top edge of the bias binding.

4. Thread the cord through the bias binding using a safety pin, turn the bag right side out and push the cord ends through the gap in the side seam.

5. Attach the beads to the ends of the cord either by threading or stitching according to your type of bead.

DOILY CUSHION
AND TABLE TOP

The doily cushion (page 59) and table top are quite different, both in design and colours, but they both use commercially-made doilies. The advantages are that you can achieve an intricate design without having to cut a stencil and can make your finished piece individual. Choose colours to match your decor.

FINISHED SIZE *Cushion*: the diameter of your chosen doily plus about 1½in (4cm). *Table top*: use an appropriate size mount so that your chosen doily fits the table's diameter.

MATERIALS

- Three or four doilies (of the same pattern attached to each other – do not separate)
- 28 count Cashel Linen in White, Ivory or Cream, the diameter of your chosen doily plus 6in (15cm)
- Chosen spray paint colour(s) (Peach and Rose were used for the cushion illustrated and Gold Leaf for the table top)
- Spray Mount adhesive
- Tapestry frame or large embroidery frame
- Cushion pad to fit your doily
- Trimmings of your choice
- DMC stranded embroidery cotton (floss) as required to match your decor

Using a doily as a stencil when spraying the fabric produces a wonderfully intricate effect.

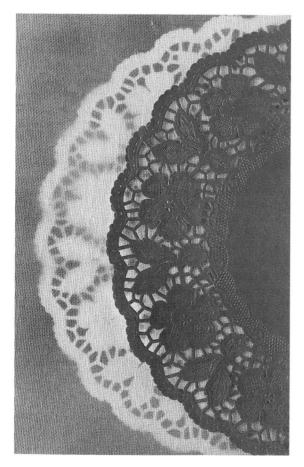

PREPARATION AND SPRAYING

1. Remove any creases from the linen and place on a flat surface.

2. Apply Spray Mount adhesive to the reverse side of your set of doilies then place in the centre of the linen. Ensure there is good contact with the linen on all edges of the doilies. If not, lift up the doilies and add more Spray Mount adhesive to them, taking care not to let the spray hit the linen direct. Re-position and press firmly but gently to achieve good contact all over.

3. Spray with your chosen paints then remove the doilies. Only the top doily will be covered with paint so, if you wish to make more than one item with the same design, you can. After the first spraying throw the top doily away and proceed with the rest.

STITCHING

All stitching is worked using two strands of embroidery cotton (floss). Mount your work in a suitable frame and use a clean copy of the doily to indicate where its flowers and leaves (or other pattern shapes) should be stitched. Try to use a combination of half-cross stitch, full cross stitch and back stitch to create variety in your design.

MAKING UP AND FINISHING

Make up as a square or circular cushion (see Making Up and Finishing for the Rose Trellis Cushion on page 30) or attach to a mount if using the design for a table top. The table illustrated was a junk shop purchase and it was renovated using decorative paper, PVA adhesive and paint. You could also renovate an old table using wood stain and/or varnish as appropriate.

TERRARIUM PICTURE

If you have worked the Flowering Bonsai Pictures on page 49 you can add this to your 'indoor garden' collection. The foliage colours range from a sharp lime green to a rich bronze, which complement the sprayed 'glass' areas. Alternatively, as it is a very decorative piece, you could use it to add colour to any room or even hang it in a shady part of a conservatory.

FINISHED SIZE framed 12 × 14in (30.5 × 35.5cm)

MATERIALS

- Two copies of the terrarium pattern photocopied onto A4 card
- 18 count Zweigart Aida in White, 12½ × 14½in (31.5 x 37cm)
- Spray paints in Rose and Lavender
- Spray Mount adhesive
- Scrap card
- Masking tape
- Embroidery or tapestry frame
- Picture mount, approximately 1½in (4cm) wide with an inner measurement of 8 × 10in (20.5 × 25.5cm)
- Suitable picture frame, inner measurement 10½ × 12½in (26.5 × 31.5cm)
- DMC stranded embroidery cotton (floss), 987 Holly Green, 989 Medium Green, 471 Green, 472 Lime Green, 746 Cream, 415 Pale Grey, 317 Grey, 3743 Pale Taupe, 209 Pale Purple, 316 Pale Maroon and 3772 Rose Brown

PREPARATION AND SPRAYING

1. Cut out the three striped areas from one copy of the terrarium pattern and spray the reverse side of the stencil with Spray Mount adhesive.

2. Remove any creases from the Aida and place it on a flat surface. Carefully place the stencil centrally on the Aida, covering the area of Aida outside the stencil edges with scrap card and masking tape. Spray with Rose paint, then remove the stencil, scrap card and masking tape.

3. Prepare the second copy of the terrarium pattern by neatly cutting around the outer edges of the dotted area and then carefully removing the black strips from inside the dotted area using sharp, small-bladed scissors. (The black areas and the main aprt of the card from which the dotted area was cut will need to remain intact because they will lie on the Aida for the second spraying. You will also need to retain the cut-out dotted area to relocate the black strips. If any piece is damaged it can be repaired using masking tape.)

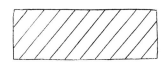

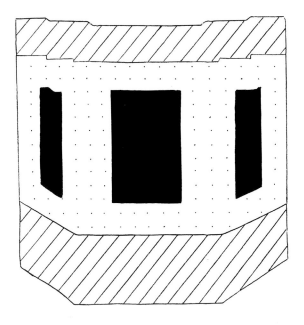

TERRARIUM STENCIL Enlarge to 140%

The spraying of the fabric for this project is a two-stage process. Carefully follow the instructions in steps 3–5 to apply the second sprayed colour.

4. Spray the reverse side of the main part of the card and the three black strips with Spray Mount adhesive. Place the main part of the card so that it joins up with the previously sprayed areas but does not overlap them. Temporarily return the dotted area to the main part of the card in order to correctly position the black strips on the Aida. Remove the dotted area to complete the second stencil.

5. Spray the Aida with Lilac paint. Remove the black strips of card.

STITCHING

All the stitching is worked using two strands of embroidery cotton (floss). Place the Aida in an embroidery or tapestry frame and stitch from the chart, working from the top to the bottom.

MAKING UP AND FINISHING

1. Remove any creases in the fabric, taking care not to iron the sprayed areas.

2. Attach your stitched piece to the backing board by the method you prefer (see page 126).

3. Place the picture mount and needlework in your picture frame.

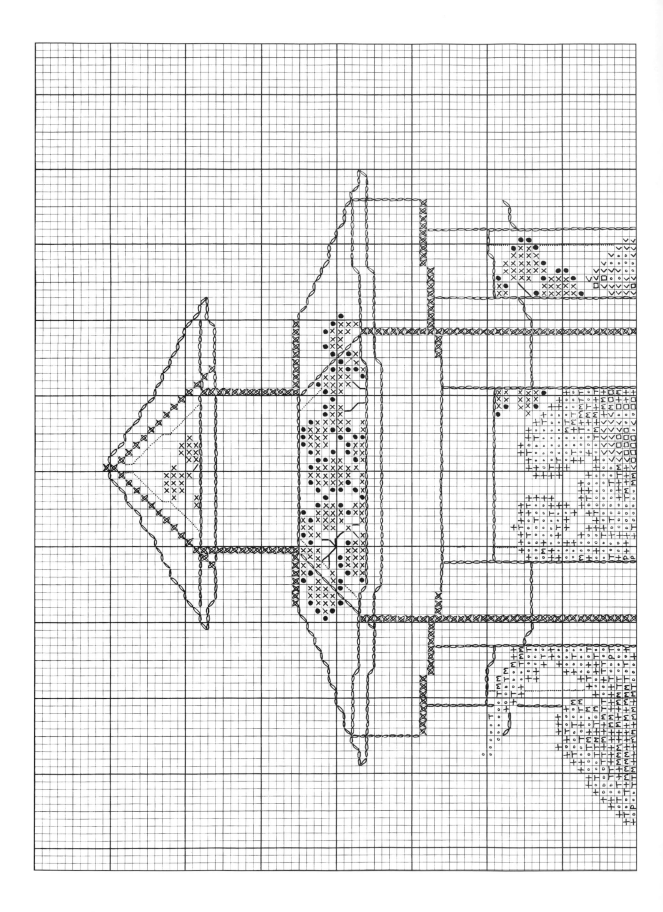

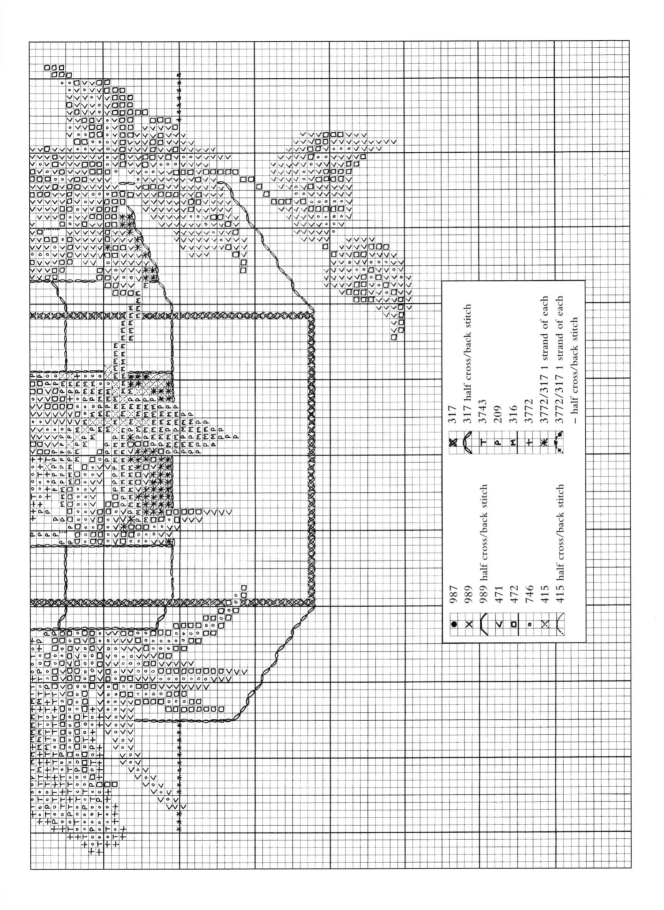

⊠	317	
⌐	317 half cross/back stitch	
⊤	3743	
ℙ	209	
ℳ	316	
+	3772	
*	3772/317 1 strand of each	
⁂	3772/317 1 strand of each	
–	half cross/back stitch	

●	987	
✕	989	
╲	989 half cross/back stitch	
⌄	471	
⊡	472	
○	746	
⊠	415	
⁝	415 half cross/back stitch	

SCULPTURE GARDEN TRAY

This project is inspired by Barbara Hepworth's Sculpture Garden, a place of tranquillity in busy St Ives,
Cornwall. It was intended that the garden and its sculptures should be viewed from holes and gaps
in other sculptures. Even the trees help to frame parts of the garden. The circular mount in this tray mimics
this idea, with a torso sculpture as the central focus. The tray is sprayed to match the texture of the sculpture.
The mount can also be covered with decorative paper or fabric to add texture.

FINISHED SIZE 9½in (24cm) square

MATERIALS

- One copy of the sculpture pattern and shadow line photocopied onto A4 card
- Spray Mount adhesive
- 18 count Zweigart Aida in Ivory, 15in (38cm) square
- Spray paints in Ceramic Blue and Black
- Embroidery frame
- Square tray (Framecraft Model WSS Tray)
- Square mount with circular centre of 6½in (16.5cm) diameter
- Silver coloured paper for covering mount (optional)
- DMC stranded embroidery cotton (floss), 3799 Dark Grey, 793 Hyacinth Blue, 3747 Sky Blue, 762 Pale Grey, 927 Pale Sea Green, 3051 Dark Green, 522 Grey Green, 989 Green, 3348 Apple Green, 3819 Lime Green, 727 Lemon, 725 Yellow, 422 Gold, 642 Bronze, 3790 Brown, 603 Deep Pink, 604 Pink and 818 Pale Pink

PREPARATION AND SPRAYING

1. Cut out the sculpture shape and the thin line below it. Spray the reverse side of the stencil with Spray Mount adhesive.

2. Remove any creases from the Aida and place it on a flat surface. Place the stencil on the Aida so that the top left-hand curve of the torso shape is approximately 1in (2.5cm) above and ½in (1.25cm) to the left of the centre point of the fabric.

3. Spray a light covering of Ceramic Blue and then spray Black down the left-hand side and around the bottom area of the sculpture, including the line below it.

4. Carefully add a few spot sprays of Black and then remove the stencil.

5. To spray the tray, detach the side of the tray by unscrewing the end screws. Remove the parts of the tray not requiring spraying.

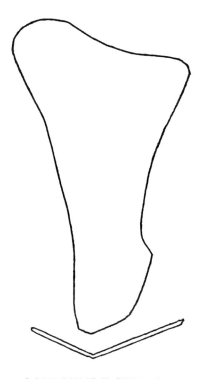

SCULPTURE STENCIL
Photocopy same size

6. The tray needs to be sprayed Black all over but you can only do this by a series of *light* sprayings. Do this over a period of several days, allowing the paint to fully harden between coats.

7. Spray a light covering of Ceramic Blue to give a speckled appearance. Spot spray with Black paint to mimic the texture of the sculpture.

8. If you are finishing the tray with a covered mount, use Spray Mount adhesive to attach the paper or fabric to the circular mount. Trim the paper back to the inner and outer edges of the mount with sharp scissors.

STITCHING

Place the Aida in an embroidery frame and work the chart using two strands of embroidery cotton (floss) throughout.

MAKING UP AND FINISHING

1. Remove the Aida from the embroidery frame and carefully iron out the creases, taking care not to apply heat to the sprayed areas.

2. Attach the stitched piece to the backing board by the method you prefer (see page 126).

3. Place the mounted work in the tray, with the mount, then add the glass (not shown in the illustration), following the manufacturer's instructions.

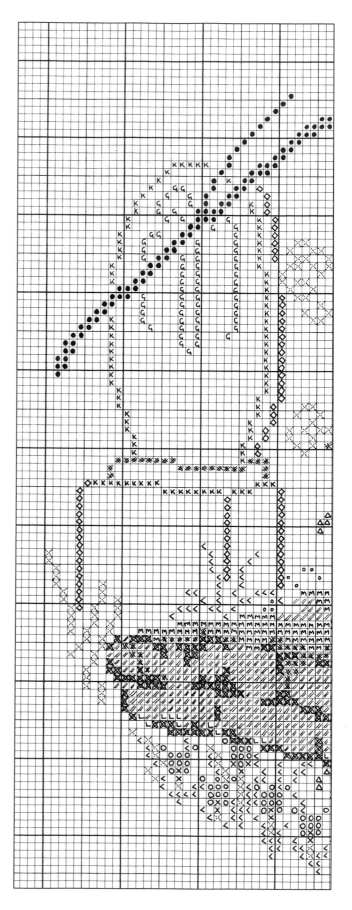

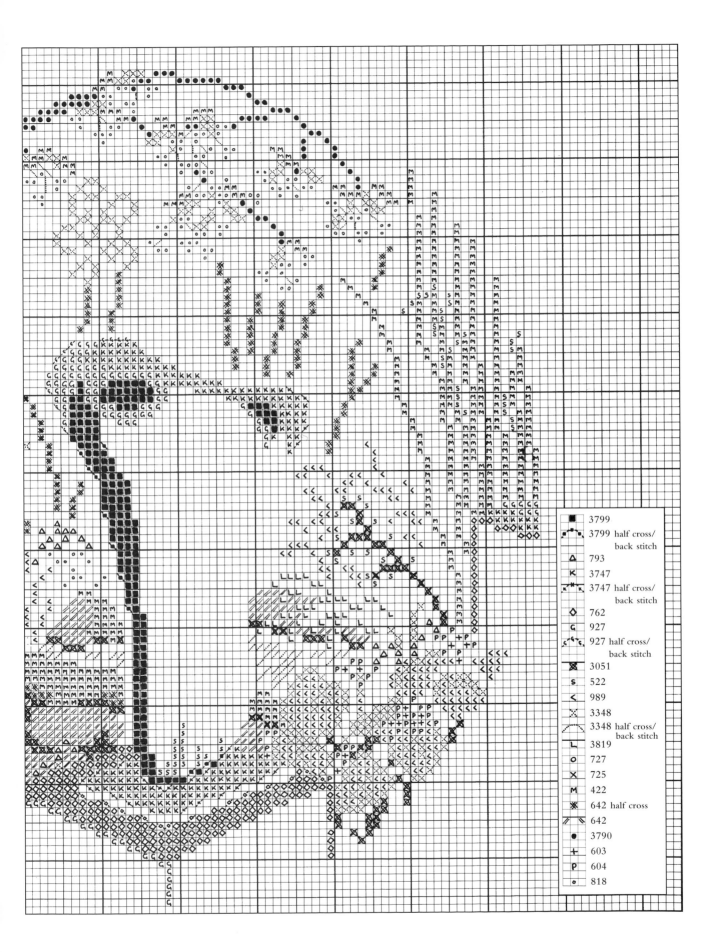

	3799
	3799 half cross/ back stitch
△	793
K	3747
	3747 half cross/ back stitch
◇	762
G	927
	927 half cross/ back stitch
⊠	3051
S	522
<	989
⋈	3348
	3348 half cross/ back stitch
L	3819
o	727
X	725
M	422
⊠	642 half cross
◿◹	642
●	3790
+	603
P	604
◦	818

TERRACE POTS BAG

This multi-purpose calico bag is ready-made with an Aida insert, making this project more simple to produce than it first seems. The pots are sprayed in four different colours, helping to create realism by adding shadow and depth to their appearance. The colourful flowers make this an attractive yet functional gift for a friend or relative.

FINISHED SIZE   14½in (37cm) square

MATERIALS

- Two copies of the pots pattern photocopied onto A4 card
- Calico bag (Framecraft, Model TBAGE)
- Spray Mount adhesive
- Scrap card
- Masking tape
- Spray paints in Dove Grey, Highland Green, Tuscan Beige and Leaf Green
- DMC stranded embroidery cotton (floss), 987 Holly Green, 989 Medium Green, 3348 Apple Green, 726 Yellow, 727 Lemon, 3706 Pink, 350 Brick Red, 102 Variegated Purple, 126 Variegated Lilac and 340 Bluebell

PREPARATION AND SPRAYING

1. Prepare both stencils by cutting out the areas marked A from one copy and the areas marked B from the other.

2. Remove any creases from the calico bag and place it on a flat surface. Slide a piece of scrap card inside the bag to cover the reverse side of the Aida (to protect the inside back of the bag from any paint seepage). Place further pieces of scrap card over the calico and secure with masking tape so that only the Aida strip is left showing.

3. Spray the reverse side of the A stencil with Spray Mount adhesive and position on the panel so that the first pot is 1⅜in (3.5cm) in from the edge of the bag. Add more scrap card if necessary.

4. Spray Dove Grey paint lightly to cover all areas of the two pots in that stencil. Then direct Highland Green at the bottom edges of the pots to create shadow and the appearance of moss-like growth. Remove the stencil.

POTS STENCIL
Photocopy same size and join two parts together at the marked points

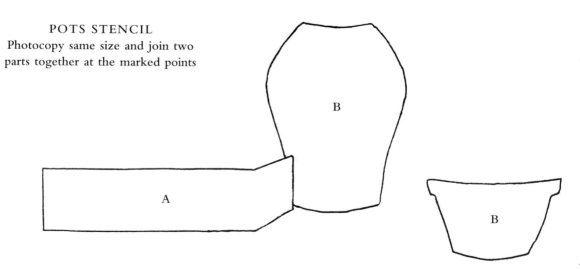

★

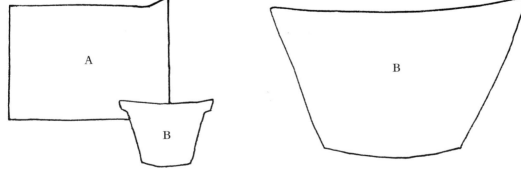

★

5. Spray the reverse side of the B stencil with Spray Mount adhesive and position it carefully on the panel so that the last pot on the right is approximately 1⅜in (3.5cm) in from the edge of the bag. If you have done this correctly two of the B stencil pots should be touching but not overlapping the two A stencil pots.

6. Spray Tuscan Beige lightly to cover all areas of the pots in stencil B. Direct Leaf Green at the bottom edges to create shadow.

7. Remove the stencil and all the masking tape and pieces of scrap card.

Photographed opposite

Top Stencil A has been sprayed as described in step 4 (page 72).
Middle Stencil B is carefully positioned and lightly sprayed with Tuscan Beige.
Below The bottom edge of the pots on Stencil B are sprayed with Leaf Green to create the impression of a moss-like growth.

STITCHING

Work the chart using two strands of embroidery cotton (floss) for all stitches. When the stitching is complete press to finish if necessary, avoiding heat on sprayed areas.

●	987		╱	3706 half cross/back stitch
X	989		⊠	350
	989 half cross/back stitch			350 half cross/back stitch
	3348		■	102
	3348 half cross/back stitch			102 half cross/back stitch
Y	726		□	126
∘	727			126 half cross/back stitch
	727 half cross/back stitch		s	340
✳	3706			340 half cross/back stitch

Allow a three-stitch gap between the two halves of the chart.

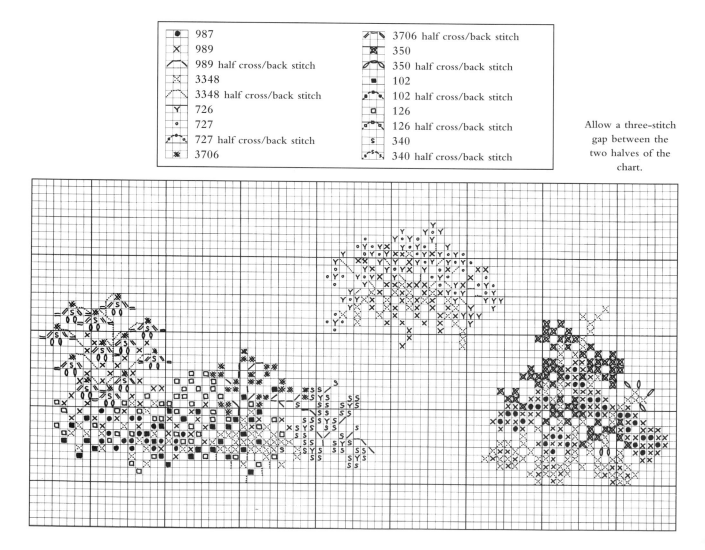

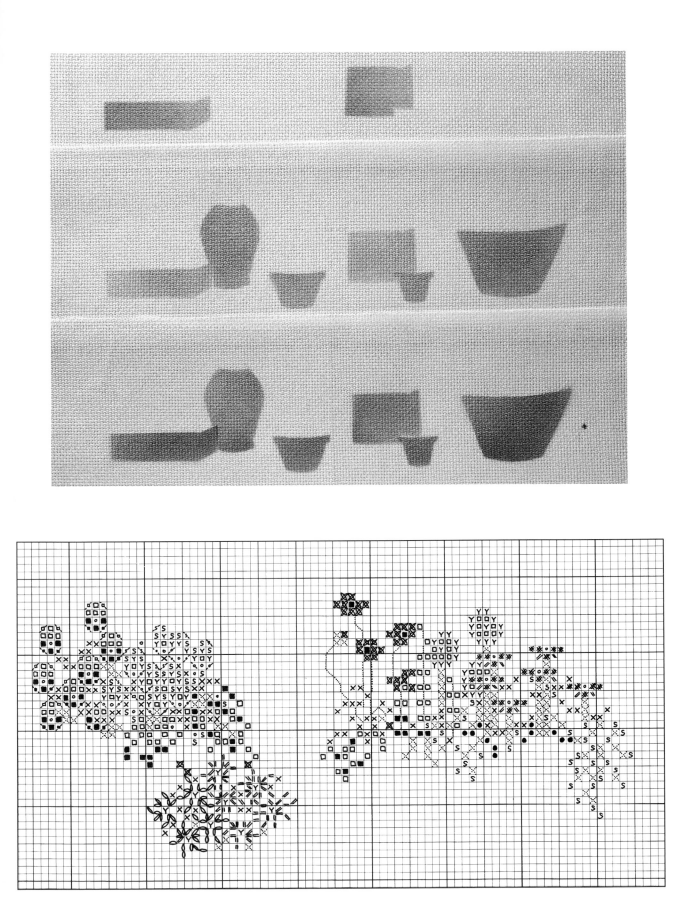

ICELAND POPPIES CLOCK

Iceland poppies come in wonderfully sunny colours and make a cheerful subject for this pretty clock. The clock-face is a simple set of divisions created with spray paint. The clock case is sprayed but you could choose another colour such as red or yellow or leave it in its original cherrywood finish.

FINISHED SIZE 7¼ × 8¾in (18.5 × 22cm)

MATERIALS

- One copy of the clock-face photocopied onto A4 card
- 18 count Zweigart Aida in White, 10 × 12in (25.5 × 30.5cm)
- Spray Mount adhesive
- Spray paints in Jasmine Yellow (plus Dove Grey, Leaf Green and Highland Green if spraying the clock-face)
- Embroidery frame
- Framecraft clock kit (Model WS Mantle)
- DMC stranded embroidery cotton (floss), 321 Dark Red, 606 Scarlet, 608 Dark Orange, 970 Orange, 741 Pale Orange, 742 Orange Yellow, 743 Golden Yellow, 727 Lemon, 3819 Lime Green, 3053 Sage Green and 3363 Green

PREPARATION AND SPRAYING

1. Cut out the black areas of the photo-copied clock-face.

2. Trim the A4 card to measure the same size as the paper dial provided in the clock kit – 5¼ × 7⅜in (13.5 × 18.7cm) – ensuring that the stencil is in the correct position. To find the correct position, place the paper dial, which has a hole in the centre, over the centre of the dial on your card. Keep in position and hold the card and paper up to the light to check that the hourly divisions correspond with each other. Make any adjustment required. Mark the corners of the paper on the card in pencil.

3. Remove the paper and using a pencil and ruler join up the corner marks to create a rectangle. Cut out this rectangle.

4. Spray the back of the card with Spray Mount adhesive. Prepare the Aida by removing any creases and placing it on a flat surface. Position the stencil onto the centre of the fabric, ensuring that the 9, 3, 12 and 6 o'clock divisions are on, and line up with, a row of holes in the Aida.

5. Spray light coats of Jasmine Yellow paint to create solid coverage. Carefully remove the stencil.

STITCHING

All the stitching is worked using two strands of embroidery cotton (floss). Place the Aida in an embroidery frame and stitch the partially open flower bud first in the position shown on the chart (page 79). (This is the bud which overlaps the clock-face.) Work the rest of the design.

MAKING UP AND FINISHING

If you wish to spray the clock as illustrated, this is best done over a period of days to give each spraying a suitable time to dry. If you are not painting the clock begin Making Up at step 2.

1. Separate the clock base from the other three sides. Use Leaf Green for the first covering (it will probably take three or four light sprayings to cover the wood finish supplied). Next use two sprayings of Dove

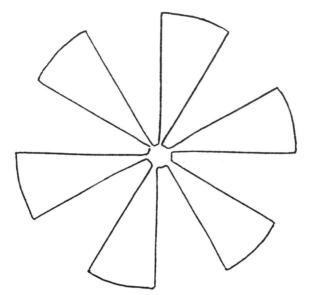

CLOCK-FACE STENCIL
Photocopy same size

Grey to give a speckled appearance. Finally, add one or two sprayings of Highland Green.

2. Remove any creases in the embroidery created by the embroidery frame taking care not to iron the sprayed area.

3. Using the yellow border as a guide, fix the design to the clock mount board by the method you prefer (see page 126).

4. Follow the kit manufacturer's instructions for cutting the centre area of the clock-face and attaching the mechanism.

5. Complete the clock by sliding the stitched piece and protective glass (not shown in the photograph on the previous page) into the grooves in the clock case. Attach the base of the clock to the clock case with the screws provided in the kit. Attach the felt pads.

Detail of the Iceland Poppies Clock stitching showing the left-hand flower-heads. The stranded embroidery cottons (floss) chosen successfully capture the wonderfully sunny colours of these delightful flowers.

Dotted line
indicates top of
spray painted
area dividing
11 o'clock and
12 o'clock

■	321
⊠	606
▲	608
⋈	970
●	741
⁄	742
▽	743
∘	727
L	3819
s	3053
x	3363

ELEPHANT FAMILY PICTURE

This elephant family and the Arabian Camels Picture on page 85 make decorative pictures for a child's room. You could also vary the mount and frame to suit other rooms. A simple stencil produces the body shapes, so the project is quick and easy to stitch. A chart is given for each elephant's apron but you could choose your own colours, making the design more individual.

FINISHED SIZE framed 18 × 11in (45.5 × 28cm)

MATERIALS

- Two copies of the elephant pattern photocopied onto A3 card
- 18 count Zweigart Aida in White, 18 × 9½in (45.5 × 24cm)
- Spray Mount adhesive
- Spray paint in Dove Grey, and a colour of your choice for the frame
- Oval embroidery frame or tapestry frame
- Air-soluble pen
- Backing board for mounting work
- Picture mount
- Double-sided adhesive tape and decorative paper (if covering the mount)
- Suitable picture frame, inner measurement 13½ × 5in (34 × 12.5cm)
- DMC metallic thread in Gold
- DMC stranded embroidery cotton (floss), 310 Black, 640 Dark Stone, 746 Cream, 726 Yellow, 740 Orange, 350 Brick Red, 666 Scarlet, 208 Purple, 792 Bluebell, 3810 Turquoise and 988 Green

To add colour and texture to your painted frame, fit strips of decorative paper, which has had lengths of narrow double-sided adhesive tape attached to the reverse side, into the grooves of the frame. Cut the ends of the strips at a 45° angle to create a mitred corner.

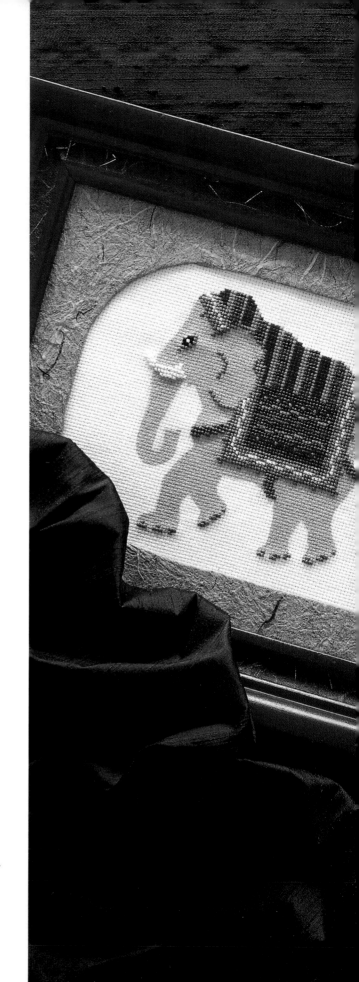

PREPARATION AND SPRAYING

1. Keep one copy of the elephants for tracing and use the other to create a stencil by cutting out the three elephants with sharp small-bladed scissors, taking great care in the areas where the elephants link up.

2. Spray the reverse side of the stencil with Spray Mount adhesive. Remove any creases from the Aida and lay it on a flat surface. Press the stencil onto the fabric so that the design is in the centre.

3. Spray a series of light sprayings of Dove Grey paint to build up a solid covering of the elephants. Remove the stencil.

4. Spray the picture frame if desired.

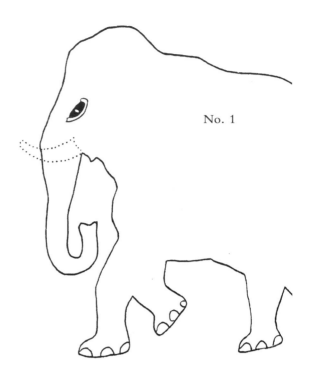

No. 1

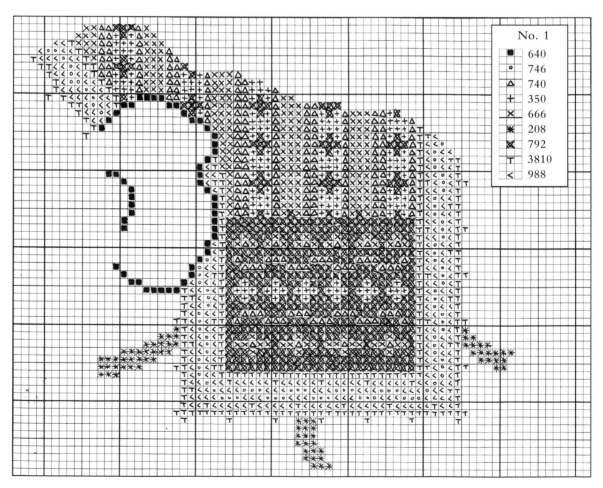

No. 1	
■	640
○	746
△	740
+	350
✕	666
✳	208
✖	792
T	3810
<	988

ELEPHANT STENCIL   Enlarge to 125%
and join two parts together

No. 2

No. 3

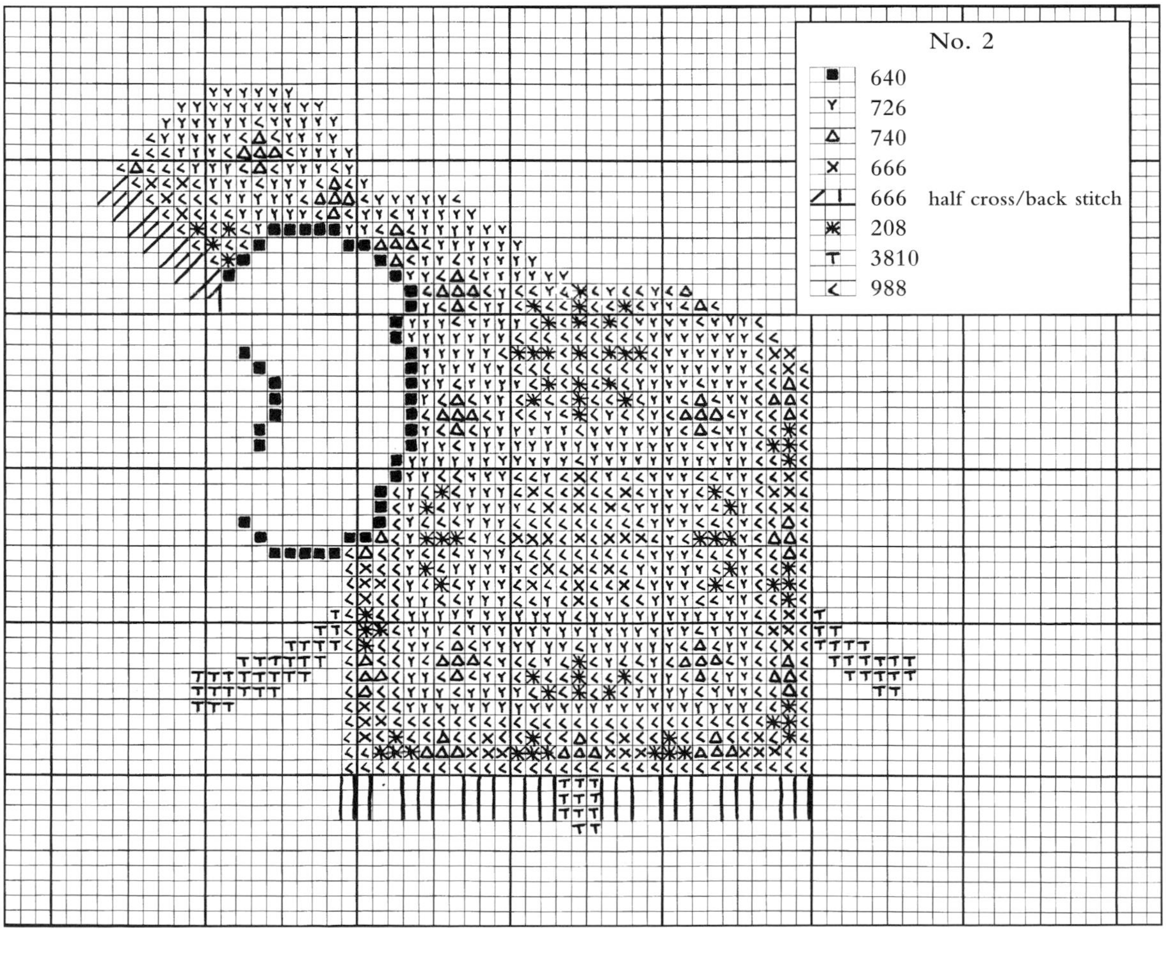

No. 2	
■	640
Y	726
△	740
✕	666
◿	666 half cross/back stitch
✳	208
T	3810
‹	988

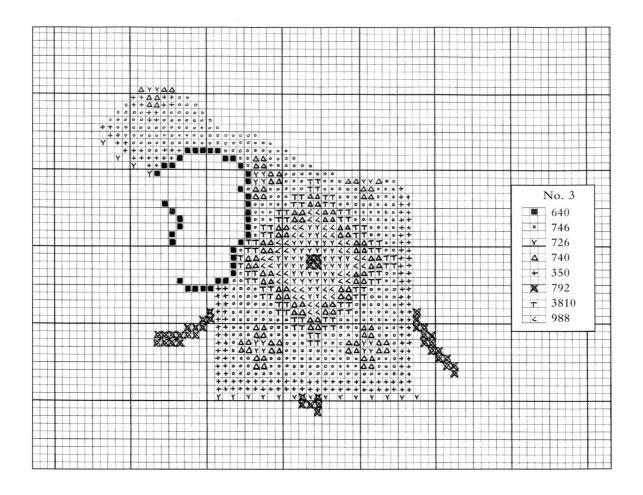

No. 3	
■	640
○	746
Y	726
△	740
+	350
✕	792
T	3810
<	988

STITCHING

All the stitching is worked using two strands of embroidery cotton (floss).

1. Place the Aida in your tapestry frame or oval embroidery frame and stitch each apron in turn.

2. Using the air-soluble pen carefully trace the position of the feet markings, the mouths, the eyes and the tusks from the uncut photocopy.

3. Stitch the feet markings and tusks in 746 Cream. (You can either use cross stitch or padded satin stitch for these areas.) Stitch the mouths using 640 Dark Stone and the eyes in 310 Black, 746 Cream and 640 Dark Stone.

MAKING UP AND FINISHING

1. If you have used a frame remove any creases, but do not iron the sprayed areas.

2. Attach the stitched piece to the backing board by the method you prefer (see page 126).

3. To cover the mount with decorative paper (if you wish to do so), cover the front of the mount with double-sided adhesive tape, placing the tape right up to, but not on, the bevelled edge (ie, the inner edge of the mount). Then, with the decorative paper face down on a flat surface, lower the taped mount onto the paper. Turn the mount over and slowly and carefully trim away the inner area with either a craft knife or sharp scissors. Place on top of your stitched piece, then frame.

ARABIAN CAMELS PICTURE

The colours in this picture reflect those used in authentic saddles, adorned with multi-coloured tassel harnesses. The use of crewel wool adds to the realism. The spraying is simple, though care must be taken with cutting and placing the stencil. The chart for the saddlecloth is provided and the rest of the detail is added, prior to stitching, using an air-soluble pen.

FINISHED SIZE framed 14½ × 10¾in (37 × 27.5cm)

MATERIALS

- Two copies of the camels pattern photocopied onto A4 card
- 27 count Zweigart evenweave fabric in Cream, 17¾ × 13¾in (45 × 35cm)
- Spray paint in Solar Yellow (plus Teal, Turquoise, Royal Blue and Highland Green if spray painting the frame as illustrated)
- Spray Mount adhesive
- Scrap card
- Masking tape
- Air-soluble pen
- Embroidery frame
- Backing board for mounting needlework
- Suitable mount
- Double-sided adhesive tape (if covering the mount)
- Decorative paper (if covering the mount)
- Suitable frame, outer measurement 14½ × 10¾in (37 × 27.5cm)
- DMC Medicis crewel embroidery wool, 8027 Lemon, 8104 Terracotta, 8106 Maroon, 8128 Dark Orange, 8129 Coral, 8136 Plum, 8207 Blue, 8303 Dark Mustard, 8313 Mustard, 8314 Pale Mustard and 8419 Green

PREPARATION AND SPRAYING

1. Keep one photocopy of the camels for tracing and use the other to create a stencil for spraying by carefully cutting around the outlines of both camels.

2. Spray the reverse side of the camel stencil with Spray Mount adhesive.

3. Prepare the evenweave fabric by removing any creases and laying it on a flat surface. Place the stencil onto the centre of the fabric, making sure that the bottom edges of the saddlecloths are parallel with horizontal threads of the fabric. Make any adjustments necessary and then press the stencil firmly onto the fabric.

4. Mask the area surrounding the stencil using scrap card and secure with masking tape.

5. Spray a solid coat of Solar Yellow. Carefully remove the scrap card and stencil.

STITCHING

Place the sprayed fabric in an embroidery frame. Use one strand of crewel embroidery wool except for the nose and neck bands which are worked in cross stitch using two strands of 8314 Pale Mustard. Each camel is worked in the same manner except for the eyes. Use an air-soluble pen to mark knees and shadow lines/areas.

Saddlecloth Following the chart and starting at the lower edge of the saddlecloth, work the patterned area using the different colour combinations for each cloth. Using 8104 Terracotta continue working up the saddle, keeping the sides straight but completing the top of the saddle by following the line of yellow paint. Stitch an 'edge' to the saddlecloth using 8104 Terracotta in back stitch over two threads of the fabric.

Saddlecloth rear tie **A** Use 8106 Maroon and add two mock tassels (see page 19) choosing from 8106 Maroon, 8104 Terracotta and 8128 Dark Orange and varying for each camel.

Saddlecloth front tie **B** Use two strands of 8314 Pale Mustard for the bands. Work two rows of mock tassels (see page 19) using 8027 Lemon, 8136 Plum, 8207 Blue, 8419 Green, 8106 Maroon, 8128 Dark Orange and 8129 Coral. Add back stitch to the edges of the 8314 Pale Mustard, using the tassel colours in a random manner.

Saddle 'handles' **C** Stitch the inner sloping edges with one row of 8314 Pale Mustard and the rest of the area in 8313 Mustard.

Lower harness neck tie **D** Using 8106 Maroon add five stitched tassels in combinations of 8128 Dark Orange, 8104 Terracotta and 8106 Maroon (vary for each camel).

Upper neck harness **E** Stitch as for **B**.

Nose-band **F** Use two strands of 8314 Pale Mustard and edge with back stitch in 8104 Terracotta. Link the ends of **E** and **F** using back stitch in 8136 Plum to create a head-rein ring.

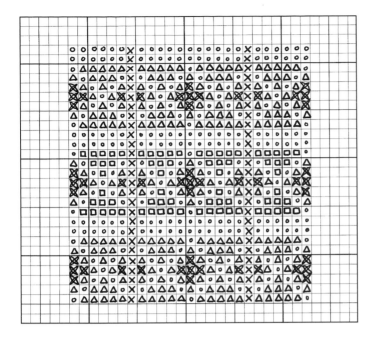

ARABIAN CAMELS SADDLECLOTH

Left-hand camel			Right-hand camel
8314	o		8303
8106	✕		8136
8128	✖		8314
8104	□		8128
8136	△		8106

Camel tails Using the mock tassel technique (see page 19) but varying the length of the stitch as well as its direction, use 8313 Mustard and 8314 Pale Mustard. Use back stitch over a single thread of fabric with 8313 Mustard along the inner length of the tail.

Rear leg shading and rear feet Working cross stitch over a single thread of fabric, and using back stitch where required (again over a single thread of fabric), use 8303 Dark Mustard, except for the piece of thigh shading just below the corner of the saddlecloth which is worked in 8313 Mustard.

Front leg shading and front feet Working cross stitch over a single thread of fabric and back stitch where required (also over a single thread of fabric), use 8303 Dark Mustard for the knee joint and all markings below. Stitch the shading above the knee joint in 8313 Mustard over a single thread of fabric.

Top back shading Work in cross stitch over a single thread of fabric in 8313 Mustard.

Face markings Work in back stitch over a single thread of fabric using 8313 Mustard.

Camel eye Work the eye on one camel only, in cross stitch and half cross stitch over a single thread of fabric using 8136 Plum.

Background dune grass Work in back stitch over two threads of fabric using 8419 Green and 8207 Blue.

MAKING UP AND FINISHING

1. Remove any creases in the fabric created by the embroidery frame, taking care not to iron the sprayed areas.

2. Attach the stitched piece to the backing board by the method you prefer (see page 126).

3. To cover the mount with decorative paper, follow step 3 in Making Up and Finishing for the Elephant Family Picture on page 84.

4. To spray the frame as illustrated in the photograph opposite, randomly spray it with successive thin layers of the paint colours given in the Materials section. Alternatively, purchase a coloured frame and add a single colour spray.

5. Place the mount and your stitched work in the frame.

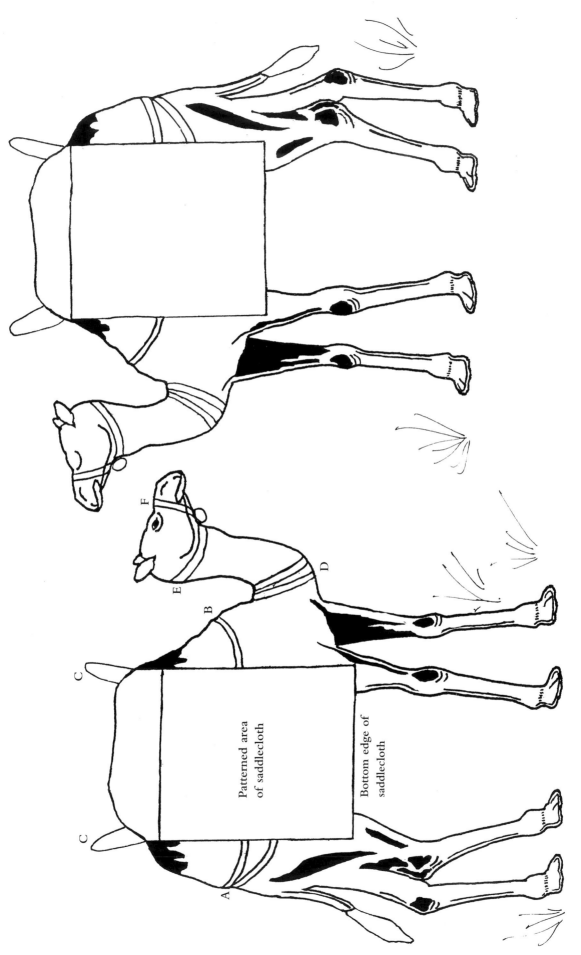

Patterned area of saddlecloth

Bottom edge of saddlecloth

A

B

C

C

D

E

F

CAMEL STENCIL Photocopy same size

CHINESE VASE WITH ANEMONES

This picture combines the wonderful shades of anemones with a vase design inspired by a Chinese Yuan Dynasty wine jar and a Chinese patterned border. The jar forms part of a collection at the Percival David Foundation of Chinese Art at the University of London.

FINISHED SIZE framed 12 × 12in (30.5 × 30.5cm)

MATERIALS

- One copy of the pattern photocopied onto A3 card
- 28 count Cashel Linen in Antique White, 18in (45.5cm) square
- Spray paints in Ceramic Blue, Rose, Sunburst Red and Lavender
- Spray Mount adhesive
- Scrap card
- Masking tape
- Tapestry frame
- Suitable picture frame, inner measurement 9½in (24cm) square

- Decorative paper to cover the frame (optional)
- DMC stranded embroidery cotton (floss), 3347 Leaf Green, 3348 Apple Green, 746 Cream, 407 Rose Brown, 304 Dark Red, 321 Red, 3721 Dull Red, 3705 Dark Pink, 899 Rose Pink, 819 Pale Pink, 602 Pale Fuchsia, 600 Fuchsia, 718 Dark Cerise, 3607 Cerise, 3608 Pale Cerise, 209 Pale Purple, 208 Medium Purple, 552 Purple, 793 Bluebell, 930 Dark Blue, 3041 Taupe and 3799 Dark Grey

Careful spraying of the vase as described in step 6 on page 93 will create shadow and depth.

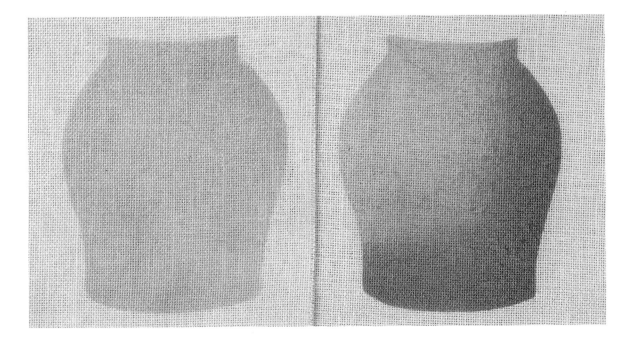

**CHINESE VASE
STENCIL**
Photocopy same size

PREPARATION AND SPRAYING

1. Cut out the flowers from the card.

2. Remove any creases from the linen and place on a flat surface. Place the stencil in the centre of the linen.

3. Cover all the areas of linen outside the stencil with scrap card and masking tape. Working from the left, spray the first flower Rose, the second Red and the third Lilac.

4. Remove the stencil but save the scrap card. Cut out the vase.

90 *Chinese Vase with Anemones*

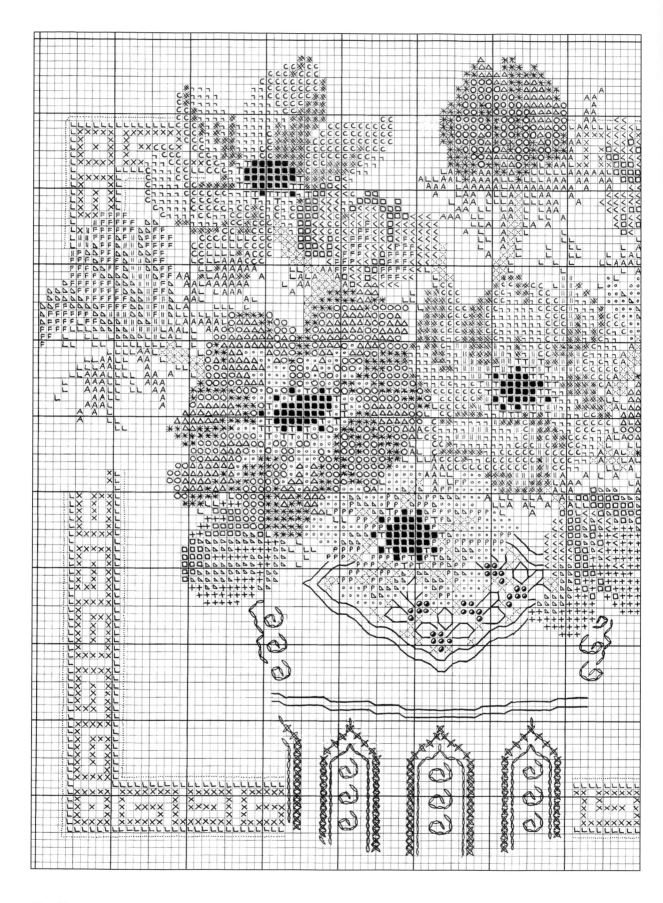

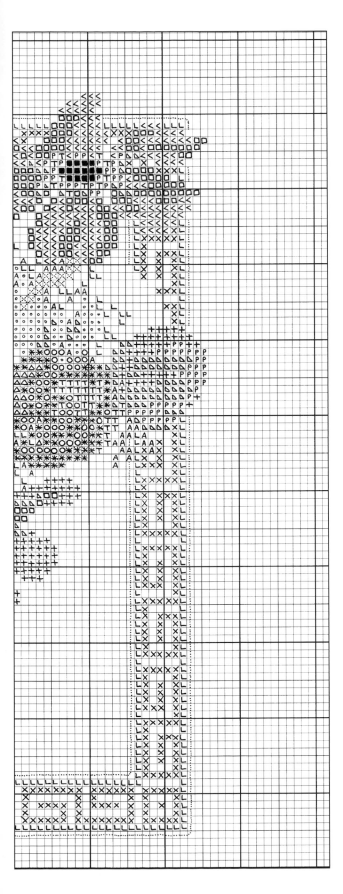

5. Apply Spray Mount adhesive to the reverse side of the stencil. Replace the stencil on the linen, lining up the sprayed flowers. Replace the scrap card and masking tape to the areas of linen outside the stencil. Cover the flowers with scrap card and secure with tape.

6. Spray the vase *very lightly* with Ceramic Blue paint. Spray again along the bottom edge of the vase and down the right-hand curved edge to create shadow and depth. Remove the stencil and scrap card.

STITCHING

1. Place the linen in the tapestry frame and using two strands of embroidery cotton (floss) work the vase pattern so that you can correctly locate and stitch the anemone flower which overlaps the vase.

2. Stitch the flowers using three strands and use a single strand for the French knots around the flower centres. Work the border last, using a single strand of thread.

MAKING UP AND FINISHING

For details of how to frame the completed piece, see page 126.

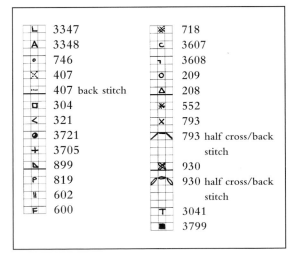

L	3347	※	718
A	3348	c	3607
∘	746	ר	3608
※	407	o	209
⋯	407 back stitch	△	208
▫	304	✳	552
<	321	x	793
◐	3721	⟋	793 half cross/back stitch
+	3705		
◣	899	⊠	930
P	819	⟋	930 half cross/back stitch
‖	602		
F	600	T	3041
		■	3799

SUN
CUSHION

Using the conventional approach to cross stitch
this cushion would take more than a week
to complete. With stencils it can be made in a few
days as only the face detail and corner motifs are
stitched. Here, a border pattern has been added but
this can be omitted. The colours could also be
altered to fit in with your colour scheme – just
match the yarns and paints to your decor. If you
wish to make a pair of cushions you could alternate
the two colours.

FINISHED SIZE 16in (41cm) square
(excluding fringing)

MATERIALS

- Two copies of the sun pattern, each photocopied onto two sheets of A3 card each (The design is too large to fit onto a single sheet of A3 so copy in two halves and join with masking tape.)
- 28 count Zweigart Cashel Linen in Antique White, 20in (51cm) square
- Spray paints in Jasmine Yellow and Royal Blue
- Masking tape
- Spray Mount adhesive
- Tapestry frame
- Backing fabric for cushion, 17½in (45cm) square
- Sewing thread to match
- Cushion fringing, 2yd (2m)
- Cushion pad
- DMC stranded embroidery cotton (floss), 334 Blue, 472 Green and 743 Yellow

PREPARATION AND SPRAYING

1. ◆ Once the two pieces for each sun stencil have been joined together trim the edges before cutting out the stencil areas. The two

SUN STENCIL
Enlarge to 180%
Cut out the yellow areas to create Stencil A, the yellow flame stencil.
Cut out the black areas to create Stencil B, the blue face stencil.

stencils have different dimensions so that the green border is created when blue is sprayed over yellow. Trim stencil A to measure 15in (38cm) square, ensuring the design is in a central position. To do this check that the outer edges of the design are equal distances from your cutting lines before actually cutting. Cut out the flames. Stencil A is used when spraying the yellow paint. To make a stencil for spraying the blue paint cut out the face and triangular shapes on the second copy of the sun pattern. This is Stencil B. Place Stencil B in position over Stencil A and trim to leave a 1in (2.5cm) border. Stencil B should now be in the correct central position and measure 13in (33cm) square.

2. Remove any creases from the linen and place it on a flat surface.

3. Spray the back of Stencil A with Spray Mount adhesive and place on the centre of the linen, make sure that you line up the edges of the card with the straight grain of the fabric.

4. Make sure the stencil has good contact with the linen and spray the cut out flames and all around the edge of the stencil with Jasmine Yellow. Remove the stencil.

5. Spray the reverse side of the blue stencil with Spray Mount adhesive and place it on the linen adjusting the position so that no yellow areas of the sun are showing and there is a 1in (2.5cm) yellow border between the edge of your stencil card and the border areas of the fabric.

6. Make sure the stencil has good contact with the linen and spray lightly with Navy Blue for the border and slightly more for the face and triangular areas. (Build up the colour in a series of short, light bursts of spray otherwise the paint will go through the weave of the linen and spread from underneath the fabric.) Remove the stencil.

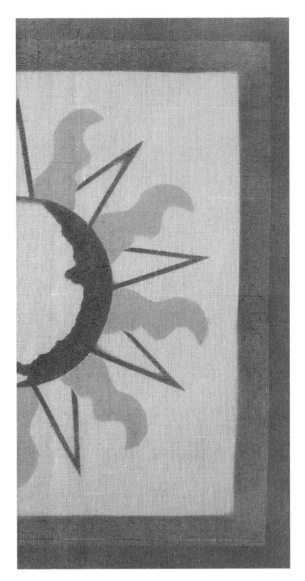

The spraying of the fabric for this project is a two-stage process. By trimming the two stencils to different dimensions a decorative double border has been achieved.

STITCHING

All the stitching is worked using three strands of embroidery cotton (floss). Mount the linen onto the tapestry frame and following the chart, work the top corners, the face and then the bottom corners. (If working the border stitch this while the linen is still on the frame. Full instructions for working the double cross stitch are given on page 19.)

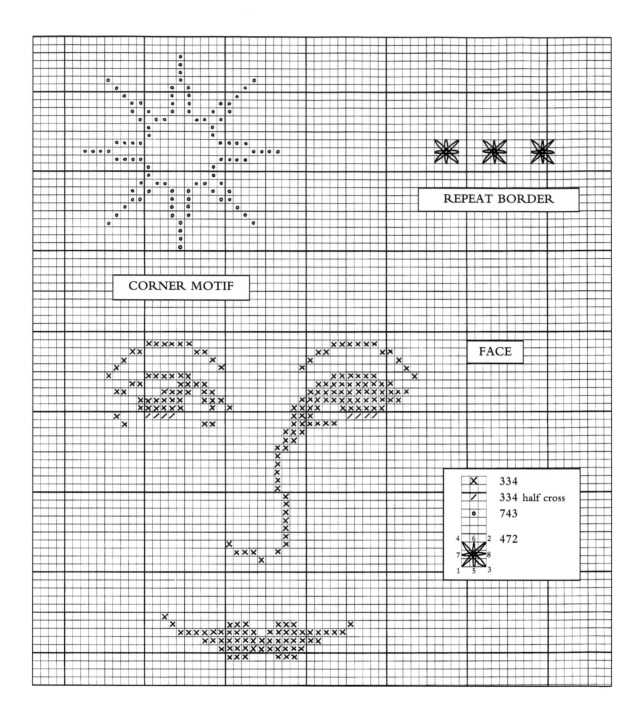

REPEAT BORDER

CORNER MOTIF

FACE

X	334
∕	334 half cross
o	743
✳	472

MAKING UP AND FINISHING

1. Remove your work from the tapestry frame and trim the linen to produce a 1¼in (3.25cm) green border.

2. Trim the backing fabric to the same size as the embroidery linen.

3. Follow steps 1 to 4 in Making Up and Finishing of the Rose Trellis Cushion on page 30. Sew the fringing on around the cushion.

4. Press the seam allowance of ⅝in (1.5cm) on the bottom edge, place the cushion pad inside and close up with small stitches of oversewing.

ROPE TWIST CURTAIN TIE-BACKS

The rope twist pattern of these tie-backs can be used in combination with most fabrics and the choice of colours can be varied to complement your curtains. If you have several windows to decorate you can always omit the cross stitch and create the tie-backs in less than a day! However, they do look more interesting with added cross stitch and the design allows you to be as creative as you wish.

FINISHED SIZE end to end 21½ × 4¾in, narrowing to 1½in (55 × 12cm to 4cm)

MATERIALS (For a single tie-back)

- ◆ Two copies of the rope twist pattern (with one printed in reverse), using a separate sheet of A3 card for each
- ◆ 28 count Zweigart Cashel Linen in Antique White, 25½ × 8½in (64.5 × 22cm)
- ◆ Spray paints in Turquoise, Jasmine Yellow and Highland Green
- ◆ Spray Mount adhesive
- ◆ Scrap card
- ◆ Masking tape
- ◆ Tapestry frame
- ◆ Interlining, size as for linen
- ◆ Backing fabric, size as for linen
- ◆ Pair of D-ring fittings (or other similar fixings/attachments)
- ◆ Piping cord
- ◆ DMC stranded embroidery cotton (floss), 3810 Turquoise, 905 Dark Green, 989 Medium Green, 472 Lime Green, 3822 Pale Gold and 3820 Gold (or your own choice of colours)

PREPARATION AND SPRAYING

1. ◆ Cut out the rope twist pattern and its reverse image from the two pieces of card. Apply Spray Mount adhesive to the reverse side of one stencil.

2. ◆ Fold the linen in half and carefully make a centre crease which will act as a guide to where the two stencils should meet. Open up the linen and place it on a flat surface.

3. ◆ Position the stencil carefully on the linen so that the wide end of the pattern is lined up with the centre crease line on the linen. Make sure that the long, straight top edge of the tie-back lies along a horizontal thread of the linen. Cover up all the linen outside the stencil with scrap card and masking tape to protect.

4. ◆ To create the effect shown in the illustration spray Turquoise paint round the

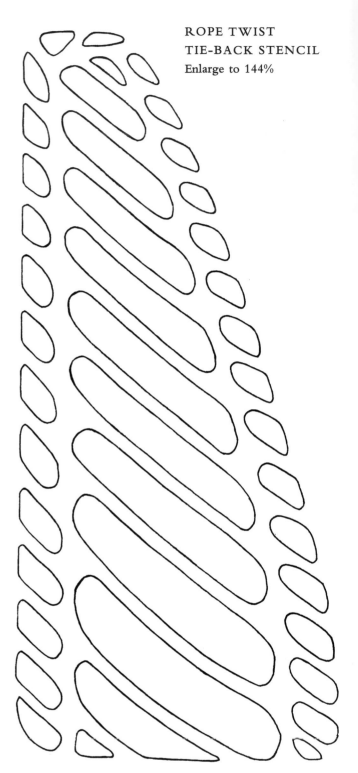

ROPE TWIST
TIE-BACK STENCIL
Enlarge to 144%

three narrow-twist border edges, spray Jasmine Yellow over the large-twist pattern and Highland Green in the gaps between the other colours. Remove the stencil and card.

The fabric, sprayed with the rope-twist pattern and its reverse image, is now ready for stitching.

5 ♦ Apply Spray Mount adhesive to the reverse side of the other stencil and position on the linen so that it creates a matching half to the first stencil. The stencil should be next to, but not overlap, the sprayed area. Make sure the straight top edge of the tie-back stencil is in line with the tie-back top edge already sprayed.

6 ♦ Cover up all the linen outside the stencil with scrap card and masking tape then repeat the spraying as in step 4. Remove the stencil and scrap card.

STITCHING

Vary the stitching by using a single strand of embroidery cotton (floss) for some stitches and two strands for others.

Place the linen in the tapestry frame and proceed to stitch. The stitching is worked in a random manner to emphasise the shape and edges of the rope-twist pattern. How much stitching you do is a matter of personal choice

but the tie-backs look better with a small rather than large amount of stitching.

MAKING UP AND FINISHING

1 ♦ Place the interlining on a flat surface, the backing fabric on top (right-side up) and the stitched piece on top of that (right-side down).

2 ♦ Stitch the seam along the edges of the tie-back following the sprayed outline of the design but leave a 9in (23cm) opening in the centre of the bottom curved edge.

3 ♦ Trim the layers back to a ⅝in (1.5cm) seam allowance and clip the seam allowance round the corners of the short ends.

4 ♦ Turn right-side out and then close the opening with neat slip stitches but leave a small gap to tuck the ends of the piping cord into the body of the tie-back. Gently press on the lining side only.

5 ♦ Attach the piping cord, and fit the D-rings, or alternative fixings, to the lining of the tie-back.

BEACH SUNSET PICTURE

Sunsets have a mystical quality, with stunning colours it is wonderful to recall. This picture shows my colours for a late-summer sunset but you could choose your own shades. To produce this picture using cross stitch alone on the 18 count fabric would take a very long time. Spraying allows you to do this in a fraction of the time and be creative in the process.

Take a freer approach to spray the background fabric of the Beach Sunset Picture. Use this photograph as a guide, but don't worry if yours ends up looking a little different.

FINISHED SIZE
framed 14 × 12in
(35.5 × 30cm)

MATERIALS

- 18 count Zweigart Aida in White, 14 × 12in (35.5 × 30cm)
- Spray paints in 'sunset' colours, eg Sunburst Red, Jasmine Yellow, Solar Yellow, Peach, Orange, Rose, Lavender, Turquoise and Highland Green
- Masking tape
- Empty adhesive tape roll, approximately 3in (7.5cm) diameter
- Tapestry frame
- Backing board for mounting needlework
- Picture mount, inner measurement 10 × 8in (25.5 × 20.5cm)
- Picture frame, outer measurement 14 × 12in (35.5 × 30cm)
- DMC stranded embroidery cotton (floss), in 'sunset' and 'shadow' colours, eg 3740 Soft Purple, 315 Plum, 316 Pale Plum, 760 Pink, 350 Red, 922 Orange, 3772 Brown, 436 Dark Honey, 3820 Gold, 676 Honey, 746 Cream, 3348 Apple Green, 320 Sea Green, 3810 Turquoise, 3808 Dark Turquoise and 317 Grey

PREPARATION AND SPRAYING

1. Remove any creases from the Aida and place on a flat surface.

2. Create a white 'border' by placing masking tape on the Aida to produce a framed area with an inner measurement of 9¼ × 7¼in (23.5 × 18.5cm). Make sure the inner edges of the tape follow along and down a line of holes in the fabric.

3. Place the empty adhesive tape roll in a slightly off-centre position, with the top edge of the circle about ¾in (2cm) from the masking tape border.

4. Direct a light spray of Sunburst Red into the upper half of the adhesive tape roll, then carefully remove the roll.

5. Spray the rest of the Aida in horizontal bands of overlapping colour, working from Orange, Jasmine Yellow and Rose (across part of the sun area), to Peach, Lilac, Peach again and Solar Yellow, until all of the Aida fabric is covered.

6. To finish the spraying, randomly spot spray with Turquoise and Highland Green. Remove the masking tape.

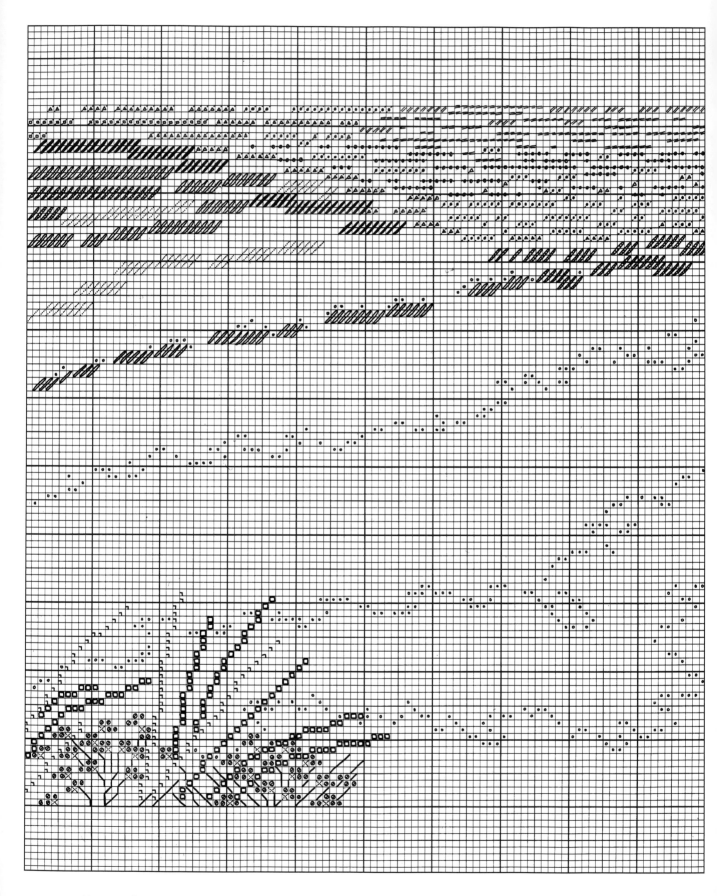

104 *Beach Sunset Picture*

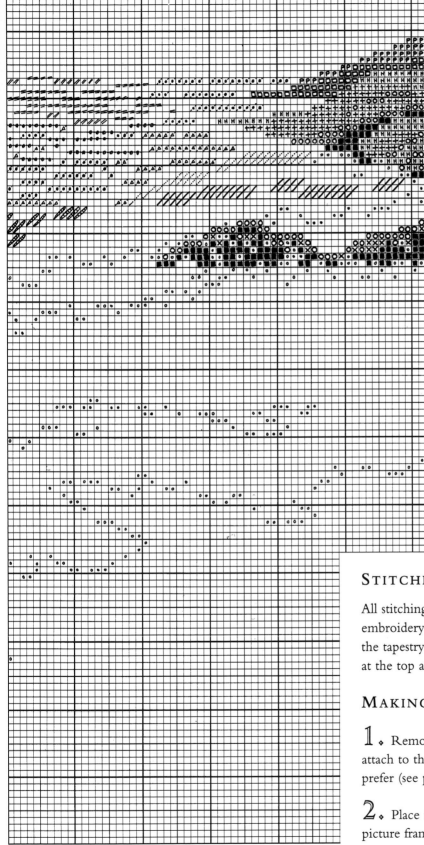

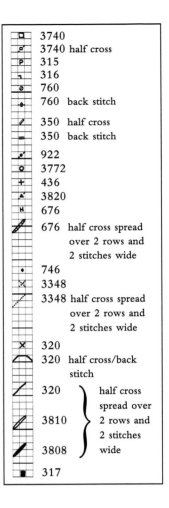

▫	3740
◢	3740 half cross
P	315
┐	316
∅	760
⊹	760 back stitch
╱	350 half cross
─	350 back stitch
∙	922
○	3772
+	436
▲	3820
H	676
╱	676 half cross spread over 2 rows and 2 stitches wide
•	746
⊠	3348
╱	3348 half cross spread over 2 rows and 2 stitches wide
✕	320
◺	320 half cross/back stitch
╱	320 ⎫ half cross spread over 2 rows and 2 stitches wide
╱	3810 ⎬
╱	3808 ⎭
■	317

STITCHING

All stitching is worked using two strands of embroidery cotton (floss). Attach the Aida to the tapestry frame and work the chart, starting at the top and working downwards.

MAKING UP AND FINISHING

1. Remove from the tapestry frame and attach to the backing board by the method you prefer (see page 126).

2. Place the needlework and mount in the picture frame.

KITTY BAG

Cats are decorative creatures and this one is functional too! Here it is used to store reusable supermarket bags. Alternatively, the bottom can be stitched closed and the elastic omitted to make a knitting bag or a bag for storing gift wrapping paper. In addition, the cat stencil can be used to decorate other items.

FINISHED SIZE 7¾ × 19in (20 × 48.5cm)

MATERIALS

- One copy of the cat pattern photocopied onto A4 card
- One sheet of Zweigart Aida Plus in Ivory
- 14 count Zweigart Aida in Black, three pieces as follows: top front 9 × 6in (23 × 15cm); bottom front 9 × 6in (23 × 15cm); back 9 × 22in (23 × 56cm)
- One piece of white lining fabric, cut to the size of the Aida Plus
- Spray paint in Black
- Spray Mount adhesive
- Scrap card
- Masking tape
- Black sewing thread
- Black elastic, about ⅓yd/m long × ⅜in (1cm) wide
- Red webbing, 1yd/m long × 1in (2.5cm) wide
- DMC stranded embroidery cotton (floss), 469 Dark Green, 470 Green, 3348 Pale Green, 734 Pale Moss, 350 Deep Coral, 606 Orangey Red, 666 Scarlet and 347 Dark Red

PREPARATION AND SPRAYING

1. Make the stencil by carefully cutting out the black areas of the card and then spray the reverse side of the stencil with a thin coat of Spray Mount adhesive.

2. Position the stencil on the Aida Plus so that the bottom left widest part of the cat and the bend in the cat's tail on the right are an equal distance from their respective edges of the fabric. (*Note*: The cat's body is off-centre. Its front paws should be level. The right ear should be slightly nearer the top edge than the bottom edge of the tail is from the bottom edge of the fabric.) Cover the outer edges of the Aida Plus with scrap card and masking tape.

3. Press the stencil firmly onto the fabric then spray a series of light sprays of Black paint to give a good solid covering. Carefully remove the stencil.

STITCHING

All the stitching is worked using two strands of embroidery cotton (floss). Start by working the geranium leaves and flowers following the chart on page 109. Commence the stitching of the right-hand side of the border by beginning the inner row at the saved square from the stencilled tail and the outer row one row of Aida above the lowest part of the tail. Work the left-hand side parallel to the right leaving five squares between the border and the tip of the tail. Lengthen or shorten the border to centralise it.

MAKING UP AND FINISHING

1. Tack (baste) your white lining fabric to the reverse side of the Aida Plus. (This lining can be ironed onto the reverse side of the Aida Plus as the heat of an iron activates the glue-based stiffening but it looks better if you tack (baste) it into position. Bear in mind that you must do take care to stitch within the seam allowance as holes made in Aida Plus are permanent.)

2. Attach the black Aida top front and bottom front panels to the stitched piece using ½in (1cm) seam allowances. With right sides together attach the back panel to the front using a ½in (1cm) seam allowance for the side seams.

3. At the top edge press a ¼in (0.5cm) turning. Turn again to create a ¾in (2cm) hem and slip stitch this hem. At the bottom edge press a ½in (1cm) turning. Turn again to create a ⅝in (1.5cm) hem. Slip stitch this hem using the black sewing thread double and leave an opening 1in (2.5cm) wide to thread the elastic through the hem. (If using the bag as a knitting bag, simply stitch the bottom edge when you stitch the side seams.)

4. Thread elastic through the bottom hem using a safety pin and adjust to a suitable length (long enough for your fingers to fit inside but not so long that the stored bags fall out). Either tie a knot or stitch the ends of the elastic to make it secure. Finish the hem and then turn the bag right side out.

5. Attach the red webbing handles, cutting them to the desired length by folding the ends and slip stitching them onto the top edge hem, taking care not to let stitches show on the right side. Press the black Aida if this is required. (The lined Aida Plus should have kept its shape but if creases do persist after hanging for a while, press the front panel gently with a warm iron. Avoid iron contact with the fabric by covering the front panel with two layers of paper and a damp cloth and then pressing with a warm iron.)

CAT STENCIL Enlarge to 120%

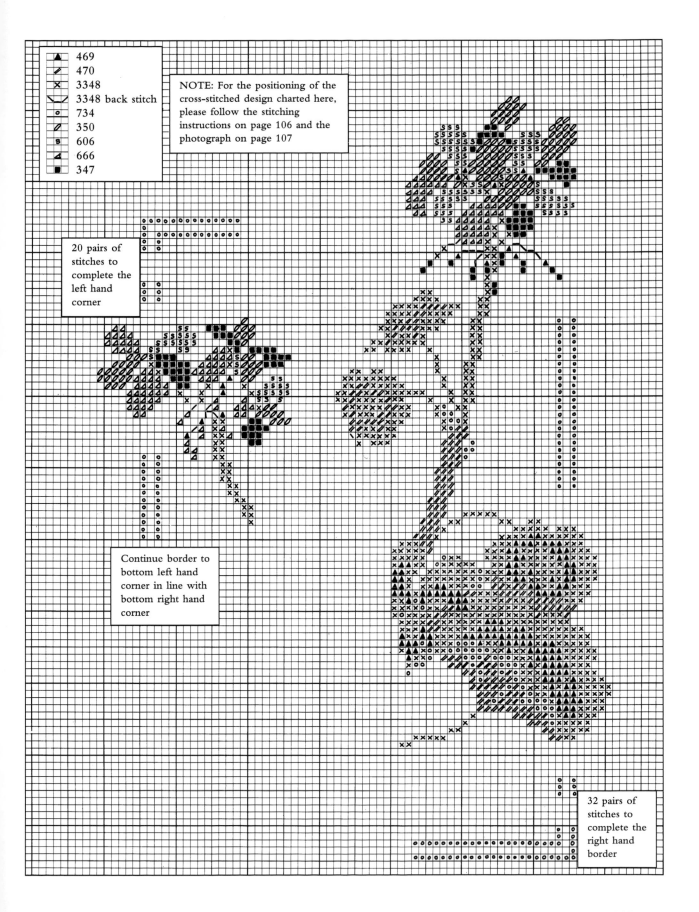

NOTE: For the positioning of the cross-stitched design charted here, please follow the stitching instructions on page 106 and the photograph on page 107

	469
	470
	3348
	3348 back stitch
	734
	350
	606
	666
	347

20 pairs of stitches to complete the left hand corner

Continue border to bottom left hand corner in line with bottom right hand corner

32 pairs of stitches to complete the right hand border

LEAFY TRAY AND NAPKINS

The warm colours of fallen leaves and seasonal fruits often have a jewel-like quality and are ideal design sources for this full-size classic serving tray. The two napkin motifs feature elements of the tray design and combine to make a very attractive set.

FINISHED SIZES tray 16 × 12in (41 × 30cm); napkins 10in (25.5cm) square

MATERIALS (For the tray only)

- Two copies of the Leafy Tray pattern photocopied onto A3 card
- 28 count Zweigart Linen in Ivory or Cream, 20 × 16in (50 × 40cm)
- Spray paints in Jasmine Yellow, Orange, Sunburst Red, Tuscan Beige and Highland Green
- Spray Mount adhesive
- Scrap card
- Masking tape
- Large embroidery or quilting frame
- Air-soluble pen
- Framecraft tray (Model WST)
- DMC stranded embroidery cotton (floss), 3726 Pale Blackberry, 3802 Blackberry, 817 Dark Red, 349 Red, 720 Dark Orange, 721 Orange, 976 Caramel, 738 Pale Caramel, 831 Dark Moss, 370 Moss, 3819 Lime Green, 472 Pale Green, 3364 Dull Green, 369 Palest Green, 727 Lemon, 743 Yellow and 3821 Gold
- *Note:* If making the napkins, each requires a piece of 28 count Zweigart Linen in Ivory or Cream, 10in (25.5cm) square and uses yarn left over from the tray

PREPARATION AND SPRAYING

1. Keeping one of the patterns for reference when stitching, cut the leafy wreath from the other to produce the outer oval border stencil.

LEAFY TRAY STENCIL
Enlarge to 124%

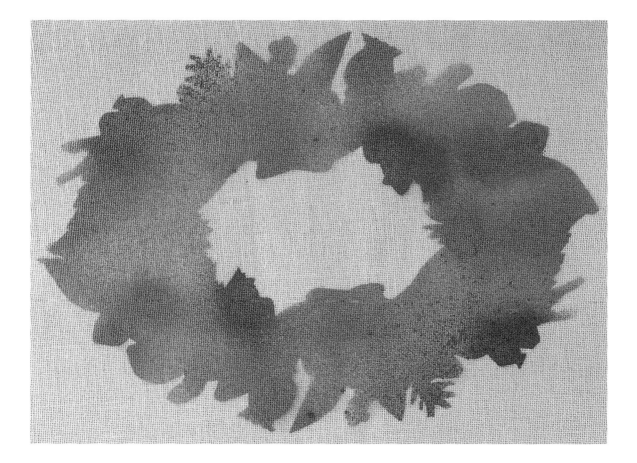

This photograph gives you some idea of what your sprayed fabric may look like before you begin stitching.

Take the cut out leafy wreath and cut the white centre area from it, taking care to keep both intact. This is important because the centre area forms part of the stencil and the leafy wreath is used to locate the centre area in the correct position. If either pieces are cut in the wrong place they can be repaired using masking tape.

2. Remove any creases from the linen and place it on a flat surface.

3. Spray the reverse side of the outer oval border stencil and the centre area piece with Spray Mount adhesive. Place the outer oval border stencil in the centre of the linen. Position the cut-out of the leafy wreath so that it matches with the outer border stencil. Place the centre area of the stencil in the middle. (The cut-out pieces of card should now look like a complete piece on the linen.)

4. Protect the linen outside the stencil card from paint by using scrap card secured with masking tape.

5. Remove the leafy wreath and make sure that all the edges of the card left on the linen have good contact with the fabric.

6. Spray the colours as indicated in stages (i)–(v) below. Do not worry about overlaps of colour or if colours go slightly astray – it all adds to the individuality of the piece.
(i) A very light spray of Jasmine Yellow all over.
(ii) Spots of Sunburst Red in the two 'hips' areas.

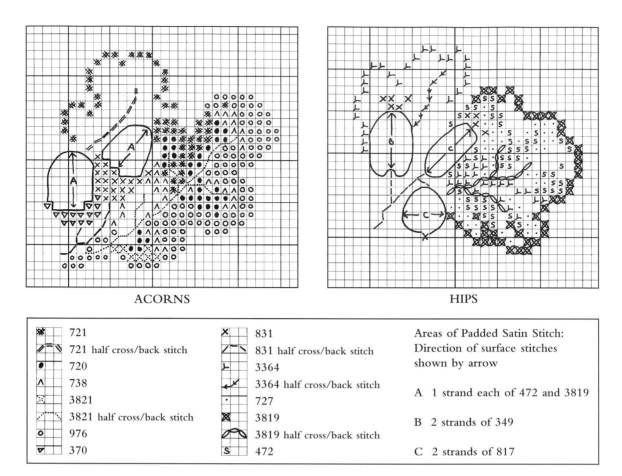

ACORNS   HIPS

✳	721		✗	831	
╱ ╲	721 half cross/back stitch		╱ ╲	831 half cross/back stitch	
●	720		⌐	3364	
∧	738		↙	3364 half cross/back stitch	
⋰	3821			727	
⋰	3821 half cross/back stitch		⊠	3819	
○	976		⌒	3819 half cross/back stitch	
▽	370		S	472	

Areas of Padded Satin Stitch:
Direction of surface stitches
shown by arrow

A   1 strand each of 472 and 3819

B   2 strands of 349

C   2 strands of 817

(iii) Spray 'strokes' of Highland Green in the acorn and bay leaf areas.

(iv) Spray Tuscan Beige on the two 'poppy seed heads'.

(v) Spray Orange over the areas not covered by colours used in stages (iii), (iv) and (v).

7. Remove the two pieces of stencil card, the scrap card and the masking tape.

STITCHING

All the stitching is worked using two strands of embroidery cotton (floss).

1. Place the linen in an embroidery or quilting frame.

2. As you work each element of the design, trace its outline from that marked on the pattern on page 112 using an air-soluble pen.

Leaves **A** Work the centre veins in 472 Pale Green, the stitched half leaves in 3364 Dull Green and the highlights (on some leaves only) in 369 Palest Green.

Leaves **B** Work in combinations of the three Yellows (727, 743 and 3821), two Oranges (720 and 721), 976 Caramel and 3819 Lime Green.

Leaves **C** Work in 743 Yellow, 3821 Gold and 3819 Lime Green.

Leaves **D** Work in 472 Pale Green, 3819 Lime Green and both Blackberry shades (3726 and 3802).

Leaves **E** Work in 976 Caramel.

Leaves **F** Work in both Caramel shades (738 and 976).

Poppy seed heads Work in 738 Pale Caramel, both Blackberry shades (3726 and 3802) and 831 Dark Moss.

Hazelnuts Work in 738 Pale Caramel for the cross stitch and 976 Caramel for padded satin stitch.

Hips Work in 370 Moss for the cross stitch tips, 3802 Blackberry for the end cross, and the lined satin stitch in mostly 349 Red, with some 817 Dark Red for shading.

Blackberries Work in 370 Moss and 831 Dark Moss for the interconnecting stitches and the fruit ends, and the flesh of the fruit in both Blackberry shades (3726 and 3802) in padded satin stitch.

Orange berries Work in padded satin stitch in both Orange shades using the darker 720 for berries in the shadow of the bay leaves.

Acorns Work in both Moss shades (831 and 370) for the cross stitch cups and stems. One strand of 3819 Lime Green is combined with one strand of 472 Pale Green for the padded satin stitch of the acorn nuts.

Sycamore seeds Work in 370 Moss for the shading cross stitch and 738 Pale Caramel for the main part of the seed's cross stitch and use straight stitch for the 'wings'.

MAKING UP AND FINISHING

Remove the needlework from the frame and attach to the backing board supplied with the tray kit. Trim any excess fabric if necessary then follow the manufacturer's instructions for completing the tray.

TO MAKE THE NAPKINS

These are simple to make and the size can be enlarged if preferred.

For each napkin, cut a piece of linen 10in (25.5cm) square and fray the edges to create a fringe measuring ½in (1.25cm). Work a motif in one corner according to the chart details. (Both motifs use colours used in the tray design.) Press to finish.

Detail of the Leafy Tray wreath design.

POND
PICTURE

Water, whether it be a river, the sea or a small pond, is difficult to portray in a realistic manner in cross stitch. Spray painting, however, makes it possible to achieve the mud-like colour seen in natural ponds and thereby produce a more realistic result. The sprayed linen is transformed into a pretty picture with the embroidery thread. For a more personal touch you can also add your own colours to the foliage surrounding the pond.

FINISHED SIZE framed 13 × 11in
(33 × 28cm)

MATERIALS

- One copy of the pond picture photocopied onto A4 card
- 28 count Zweigart Cashel Linen in Ivory, 16 × 14in (40.5 × 35.5cm)
- Spray paints in Ceramic Blue, Parrot Green, Tuscan Beige and Leaf Green
- Tapestry frame
- Backing board for mounting needlework
- Picture mount, inner measurement 10 × 8in (25.5 × 20.5cm)
- Suitable picture frame, outer measurement 13 × 11in (33 × 28cm)
- DMC stranded embroidery cotton (floss), 986 Bottle Green, 905 Lincoln Green, 988 Medium Green, 471 Green, 3348 Apple Green, 472 Lime Green, 372 Sage Green, 832 Antique Gold, 869 Brown, 3790 Donkey Brown, 726 Yellow, 727 Lemon, 746 Cream, B5200 White, 3743 Pale Taupe, 316 Pale Maroon and 3716 Pink

POND STENCIL
Enlarge to 120%

PREPARATION AND SPRAYING

1. Cut out the water section of the pond from the photocopied card.

2. Remove any creases from the linen and place on a flat surface. Place the stencil in the centre of the linen. No Spray Mount adhesive is needed as a 'soft' edge to the water is required.

3. Spray Ceramic Blue paint over the bottom half of the pond area and Leaf Green over the top half.

4. Spray Tuscan Beige for the bulrush reflection, just right of the centre of the pond.

This photograph gives you some idea of what your sprayed fabric may look like before you begin stitching. Remember this is just a guide, so don't worry if yours looks a little different.

5. Remove the stencil and scrap card. Lightly spray Parrot Green all over the linen. Add some Leaf Green in the bottom left-hand corner.

STITCHING

All the foliage stitching is worked using three strands of embroidery cotton (floss) and the reflections use a single strand.

Attach the linen to the tapestry frame and work the chart, adding any colours you wish.

MAKING UP AND FINISHING

1. Remove the linen from the tapestry frame and attach to the backing board by the method you prefer (see page 126).

2. Place the needlework and mount in the picture frame. (If you wish to do so, you can spray the frame.)

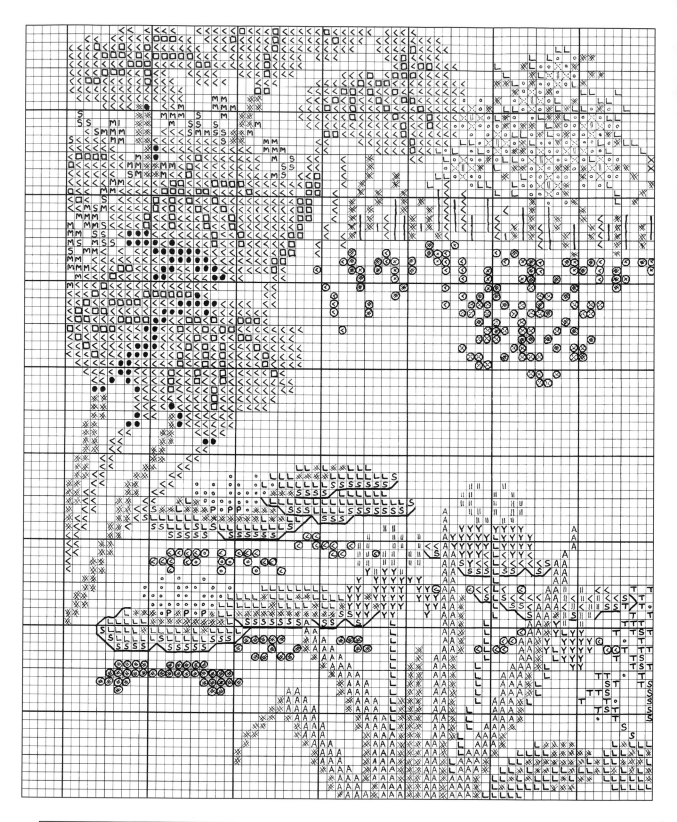

	986		372		746
	905		832		746 half cross/back stitch
	988		832 half cross/back stitch		B5200
	471		869		3743
	471 half cross/back stitch		869 half cross/back stitch		316
	3348		726		3716
	472		727		3716 French knots

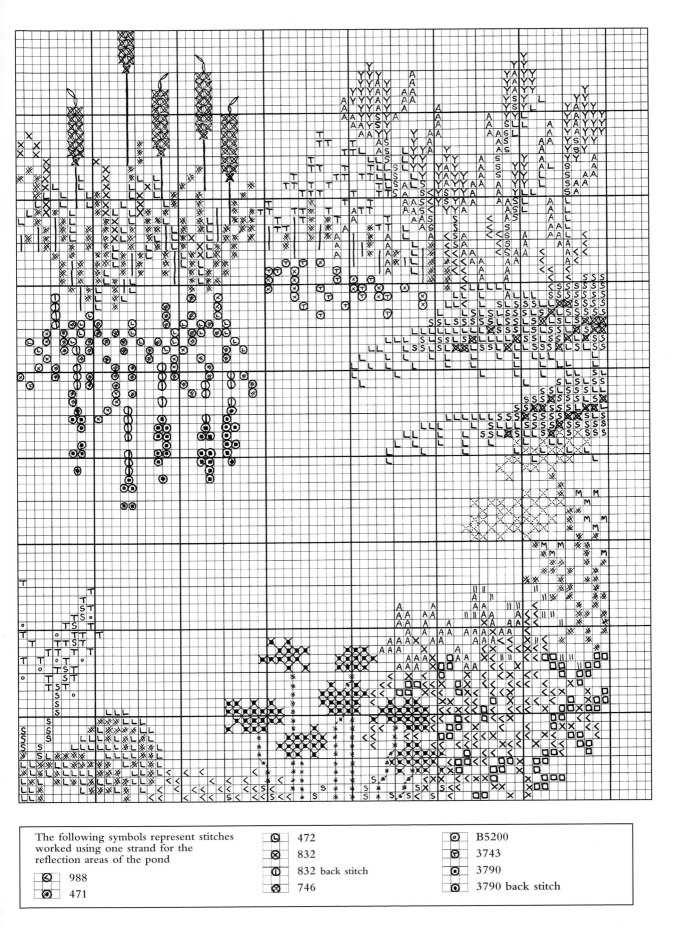

The following symbols represent stitches worked using one strand for the reflection areas of the pond

988	472	B5200
471	832	3743
	832 back stitch	3790
	746	3790 back stitch

CELTIC
CIRCLE
CUSHION

This cushion looks impressive even before you begin to stitch! You can also use the stencil on its own to decorate the centre of a table-cloth or to add colour to plain curtains. You can also vary the colours to match your own decor. Whichever way you use it (including as a circular piece, rather than as a square cushion), the projects will take surprisingly little time to complete.

FINISHED SIZE 13in (33cm) square

MATERIALS

- One copy of the Celtic circle photocopied onto two sheets of A3 card (the design is too large to fit onto one piece so join the two pieces using masking tape)
- 28 count Zweigart Cashel Linen in Ivory, 18in (45.5cm) square
- Spray paints in Highland Green and Leaf Green
- Spray Mount adhesive
- Tapestry frame
- Backing fabric for cushion, 14½in (37cm) square
- Cushion pad
- Cord, 2½yd (2¼m)
- Tassels (2–8 according to preference)
- DMC stranded embroidery cotton (floss), 988 Green, 368 Pale Green, 746 Cream, 676 Gold, 922 Orange, 350 Brick Red and 347 Red

PREPARATION AND SPRAYING

1. Prepare the Celtic Circle stencil by carefully cutting out all the black areas of the design. Spray the reverse side of the stencil with Spray Mount adhesive.

CELTIC CIRCLE STENCIL   Enlarge to 200%

2. Remove any creases from the linen and place it on a flat surface. Locate the stencil in a central position on the fabric, making sure it is in direct contact with all parts of the linen by pressing firmly.

3. Spray the outer part of the circle and spare fabric with Highland Green. Spray the centre with Leaf Green, then carefully remove the stencil.

STITCHING

1. Attach the linen to the tapestry frame and work the centre motif as given in chart A using three strands of embroidery cotton (floss) for the stitches.

2. Work the swirls and the other inner circle areas as given in chart B but using two strands of cotton (floss).

3. Repeat the motif in chart A in each corner of the cushion using three strands of embroidery cotton (floss).

4. Stitch the border pattern using chart C, and using single strands of cotton (floss).

MAKING UP AND FINISHING

Make up and finish as for the Sun Cushion on page 98.

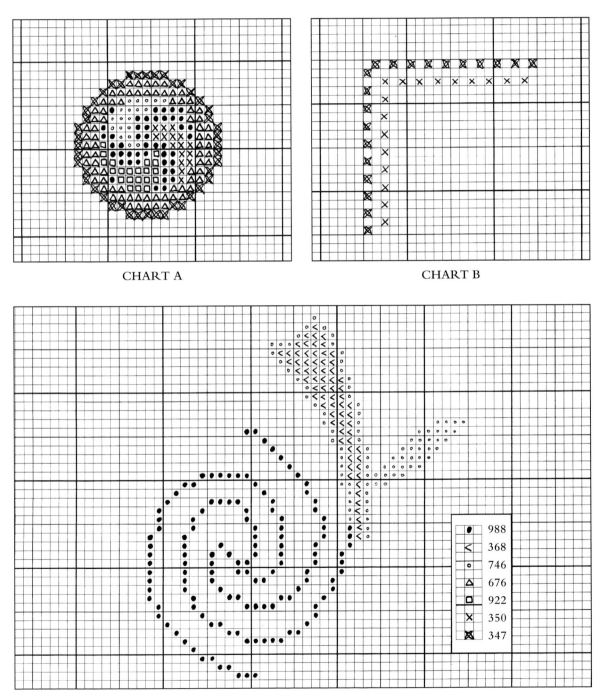

CHART A

CHART B

●	988
<	368
○	746
△	676
▢	922
✕	350
✖	347

CHART C

FRAMING ADVICE

Many of the items in this book require framing and the first step is to mount the stitched work onto a piece of backing board. A commercial framer will be able to do this for you as part of their service, although you may prefer to do it yourself. It is important that the work is mounted on acid-free board to avoid yellowing of the board, and fabric, with age. (Do not use self-adhesive blocking boards.) Instructions are given below for methods of mounting work. Lacing is the most appropriate method for mounting Aida, and using double-sided adhesive tape on the reverse side of your mount board is most suitable for linen.

MOUNTING WORK BY LACING

1. Trim any excess thread from the back of your work.

2. Most pieces should have been worked on a tapestry frame and therefore be crease-free. However, if the fabric is creased on removal from the frame, place it between two sheets of thick paper and using a damp cloth and a warm iron, press gently any creased areas. Leave the fabric on the ironing surface to cool.

3. Place the fabric on top of the backing board and manoeuvre it into a central position to create an even border around your stitching.

4. Place a dressmaker's pin through the fabric and the centre of the edge of the backing board on each of its four dimensions. Check that the fabric is in the correct position and adjust if required.

5. On one edge of the board, working towards the corners, place more pins at roughly ½in (1cm) intervals. Repeat this process at the opposite edge, ensuring that the fabric threads are straight.

6. Using either polyester thread double, or a single strand of button thread, lace together at the back of the card the end pieces of fabric

of the two shortest sides. Start and finish the lacing approximately 1½in (4cm) away from the corners. Remove the pins.

7. Repeat steps 5 and 6 on the two longest sides. Mitre the corners to keep the work neat and avoid bulkiness.

MOUNTING WORK USING DOUBLE-SIDED ADHESIVE TAPE

1. Place strips of double-sided adhesive tape along all four sides of the back of the mount board, as close to the edge as possible.

2. Follow steps 1 to 5 of the lacing instructions above and repeat step 5 so that all four edges are pinned.

3. Peel the protective strip from one piece of tape and press the fabric firmly to the tape. do the same at the opposite edge and then the remaining two edges.

4. Mitre the corners by carefully lifting the fabric away from the tape at the corners and gently re-firming into a mitred position. Finish by trimming all excess fabric.

The mounted work can now be placed in the frame, with your chosen mount, if appropriate. Other finishing information of a more specific nature is provided alongside individual projects.

Suppliers

The paints used in the projects in this book are widely available from DIY or hardware stores and car accessory shops.

The enamel paints are all from Plasti-kote's Odds N Ends range, further information can be obtained from:

Plasti-kote Ltd
London Road Industrial Estate
Sawston
Cambridgeshire
England
CB2 4TR
Tel: 01223 836400
Fax: 01223 836686

Plasti-kote
PO Box 708
1000 Lake Road
Medina
Ohio 44258 070
USA
Tel: 800 251 4511

The professional car touch-up paints are available from Halfords in the UK and similar suitable paints can be obtained in automobile accessory stores in the USA. For futher information about the particular paints used in this book contact:

Hycote Ltd
Salmon Fields
Royton
Oldham
OL2 6HZ
England
Tel: 0161 627 1066

For a wide range of stranded cotton (floss), yarns and fabrics, and items such as greeting card blanks contact:

DMC Creative World Ltd
Pullman Road
Wigston
Leicestershire
LE18 2DY
England
Tel: 0116 281 1040
Fax: 0116 281 3592

The DMC Corporation
Port Kearny
Building 10
South Kearny
New Jersey 07032
USA
Tel: 201 589 0606
Fax: 201 589 8931

DMC
51-66 Carrington Road
Marrickville
New South Wales 2204
Australia
Tel: 2 559 3088
Fax: 2 559 5338

S.A.T.C.
43 Somerset Road
PO Box 3869
Capetown 8000
South Africa
Tel: 21 41 98040
Fax: 21 41 98047

For items for finishing the projects, including wooden bell pull ends, trays, the calico bag and clock, and a range of picture frames contact:

Framecraft Miniatures Ltd
372–376 Summer Lane
Hockley
Birmingham
B19 3QA
England
Tel: 0121 212 0551
Fax: 0121 212 0552

Overseas Distributors
The following distributors may not currently have the full range of products. If you have difficulties obtaining any of the items you need contact Mike Gray, Managing Director, at Framecraft Miniatures for information.

Anne Brinkley Designs Inc
12 Chestnut Hill Lane
Lincroft
NJ 07738
USA
Tel: 908 530 5432
Fax: 908 530 3899

Gay Bowles Sales Inc
PO Box 1060
Janesville
WI 53547
USA
Tel: 608 754 9212
Fax: 608 754 0665

Ireland Needlecraft Pty Ltd
4, 2–4 Keppel Drive
Hallam
Vic 3803
Australia
Tel: 3 702 3222
Fax: 3 702 3255

Duraplast Distributors Inc
PO Box 75279
White Rock
British Columbia V4A 9N4
Canada
Tel: 604 536 2251
Fax: 604 536 2251

The Embroidery Shop
286 Queen Street
Masterton
New Zealand
Tel: 6 377 1418
Fax: 6 377 1418

INDEX